6/10

TONY HAWK

By Mike Kennedy

People We Should Know

Gareth Stevens
Publishing

Please visit our web site at **www.garethstevens.com**.
For a free color catalog describing our list of high-quality books,
call 1-800-542-2595 (USA) or 1-800-387-3178 (Canada). Our fax: 1-877-542-2596

Library of Congress Cataloging-in-Publication Data
Kennedy, Mike (Mike William), 1965–
    Tony Hawk / by Mike Kennedy.
        p. cm. — (People we should know)
    Includes bibliographical references and index.
    ISBN-10: 1-4339-1952-4   ISBN-13: 978-1-4339-1952-7 (lib. bdg.)
    ISBN-10: 1-4339-2191-X   ISBN-13: 978-1-4339-2191-9 (soft cover)
    1. Hawk, Tony—Juvenile literature. 2. Skateboarders—United States—Biography—
    Juvenile literature. I. Title.
    GV859.813.H39K46 2010
    796.22092—dc22 [B]   2009003766

This edition first published in 2010 by
Gareth Stevens Publishing
A Weekly Reader® Company
1 Reader's Digest Road
Pleasantville, NY 10570-7000 USA

Executive Managing Editor: Lisa M. Herrington
Senior Editor: Brian Fitzgerald
Senior Designer: Keith Plechaty

Produced by Editorial Directions, Inc.

Art Direction and Page Production: The Design Lab

Picture credits
Cover and title page: Cover and title page: Matt Stroshane/Getty Images; p. 5: David Leeds/
Getty Images; p. 6: AP Photo/Victoria Arocho; p.7: Tom Hauck/Getty Images; p. 8, 13, 14, 16,
21: Grant Brittain; p. 9: Frazer Harrison/Getty Images for Spike TV; p. 11: Richard Mackson/
Sports Illustrated/Getty Images; p. 17: Nick Laham/Getty Images; p. 19: Yearbook Library; p.
22: John Storey/Time & Life Pictures/Getty Images; p. 25: Tim Rue/Corbis; p. 27: Nathaniel
Welch/Corbis; p. 28: Mark Epstein/Getty Images; p. 31: Getty Images; p. 33: Marcel Noecker/
Sygma/Corbis; p. 35: Matt A. Brown/X Games IX/NewSport/Corbis; p. 36, 37: Rick Rickman/
NewSport/Corbis; p. 39: Peter Read Miller/Sports Illustrated/Getty Images; p. 40: FOX/
Photofest; p. 41: Noel Vasquez/Getty Images; p. 42: Shane Gritzinger/FilmMagic; p. 43: Scott
Wintrow/Getty Images

Printed in the United States of America

1 2 3 4 5 6 7 8 9 14 13 12 11 10

Words in the glossary appear in **bold** type
the first time they are used in the text.

CHAPTER 1

The Birdman

Tony Hawk stood at the edge of the **half-pipe**. The fans at the 1999 X Games rose to their feet. So did the rest of the skateboarders in the Best Trick competition. They all felt the electricity in the air.

Hawk usually stays cool, but his **adrenaline** was pumping like never before. Everyone wondered the same thing. Could he pull off the first **900** in competitive skateboarding history? A 900 is two and a half turns—900 degrees—in midair. It is one of the hardest tricks in the sport.

Hawk competes in the finals of the 1999 X Games.

Turn, Baby, Turn

Hawk took a deep breath, pushed off with his back foot, and bolted down the **ramp**. He needed to build up as much speed as possible. That was the only way he could soar high enough to complete the two and a half turns.

The excitement of the fans energized Hawk. They wanted him to land the 900 as much as he did. Hawk rose in the air, spun once, twice, and then made his final half-turn. Still connected to his board, he dropped back to the ramp.

Fast Fact

Hawk missed the 900 twice at the 1999 X Games before he landed his third attempt.

Hawk celebrates his successful 900—the first landed in competition.

Perfect Landing

Hawk lost his balance for a moment but regained it just as quickly. He did it! He was the first skateboarder ever to complete a 900 in competition.

The crowd roared its approval. Hawk's fellow skateboarders cheered just as loudly. Everyone knew they had witnessed history. Tony raised both arms in victory. "That was my greatest personal achievement," he said. "This is the best moment of all time."

First in Flight

That's saying a lot for the guy known as the best skateboarder ever. Hawk discovered the sport when he was a kid. In the more than three decades since, he has won dozens and dozens of titles and invented just as many tricks. Few things are more important to Hawk than skateboarding. He once said, "I consider skateboarding an art form, a lifestyle, a sport."

Fast Fact

Hawk estimates that he has invented close to 100 tricks.

A huge crowd of fans watches as Hawk competes in the 1998 X Games.

Chairman of the Board

Everyone in skateboarding knows Hawk as the Birdman. Why do they call him that? His nickname comes from the way he flies through the air on his board.

What's also true is that no one has taken skateboarding to greater heights. Hawk has traveled around the world. He has fans in every corner of the globe. Indeed, skateboarding is flying higher than ever because of the Birdman.

Hawk's high-flying ways have earned him the nickname Birdman.

8

Game Time

In 1999, Hawk introduced his own video game, *Tony Hawk's Pro Skater*. Many versions of the game have been released over the years. *Pro Skater* is one of the most popular videos games ever. Players love the graphics and the tricks they can perform on the screen. The game's soundtrack is another big selling point. So are the game's characters, which include fellow skateboarders Bob Burnquist, Bucky Lasek, Elissa Steamer, and of course, Hawk.

Hawk poses at the Spike TV 2006 Video Game Awards, where he earned a trophy for Best Individual Sports Game.

Busy Man

Hawk has also started several different companies and become a successful businessman. One of his companies makes skateboarding equipment. Another makes skateboarding clothing. Hawk has his own series of video games, and he runs a movie company, too.

That's not all. He has starred on TV and in movies. He has written best-selling books. Hawk says that his favorite "job," however, is being a husband and father.

CHAPTER 2

Getting on Board

Back in the 1970s, skateboarding did not have a good reputation. It was seen as a sport for **rebels**. Skateboarders actually enjoyed being viewed this way. They were protective of their sport.

However, some people wanted to ban skateboarding. Parks designed specifically for the sport did not exist. Few companies made skateboarding equipment. If skateboarding continued on this path, it would have no future. Tony Hawk came along at exactly the right time.

Tony stands with his parents, Frank and Nancy Hawk.

Bad Boy

Anthony Frank Hawk was born on May 12, 1968, in San Diego, California. Everyone called him Tony. His parents, Frank and Nancy, already had three children: Lenore, Patricia, and Steve. The Hawk home was always alive with activity. Frank and Nancy encouraged their kids to pursue anything that interested them.

That was where Tony ran into trouble. As a child, he was a bundle of energy. Focusing on one thing at a time was nearly impossible for him. He frustrated Frank and Nancy with his bad behavior and poor grades in school. They thought sports would be a good outlet for him. Tony tried swimming and baseball, but neither one captured his imagination.

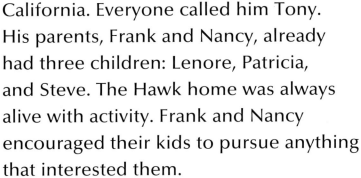

Fast Fact

Tony took violin lessons when he was a kid.

Saved by Skateboarding

No one was able to connect with Tony quite like his brother, Steve. Though Steve was much older, the two shared a close bond. Steve liked to surf, and he also did some skateboarding. Tony was eager to follow in his brother's footsteps. He got his chance when Steve gave him his first skateboard.

Nine-year-old Tony's life changed overnight. He was a natural on a skateboard. Most riders needed weeks or months to learn new tricks. Tony mastered them in a day. He couldn't get enough of the sport. His parents were both amazed and relieved. Tony seemed like a new kid. His behavior and his grades improved.

> **"**I told my dad, 'I don't want to play other sports anymore. I just want to skateboard.'**"**
>
> –Tony Hawk

Tony works on a trick as a teenager in 1981.

League of Their Own

Before long, Tony was spending every afternoon at a skate park called Oasis. He and his friends experimented with new moves. Tony developed a style of his own. His best tool was his creativity. He thought up tricks that no one else even imagined.

Frank watched his son with great pride. Tony clearly had tremendous skill. Frank wanted to make sure Tony's talent didn't go to waste. In 1980, Frank launched the California Amateur Skateboard League. The league hosted competitions all over the San Diego area. Tony won most of them.

Fast Fact

Frank Hawk flew bomber jets in World War II (1939–1945) and in the Korean War (1950–1953).

Members of the Bones Brigade pose for a photo in 1986 (left to right): Adrian Demain, Ray Underhill, Kevin Harris, Rodney Mullen, Per Welinder (hidden), Eric Sanderson, Steve Caballero (front), Tony Hawk, Mike McGill, and Lance Mountain

Dog Days

It didn't take long for news of Tony's reputation to spread throughout the skateboarding community. A company in northern California called Dogtown offered to be his sponsor. That meant Tony would be paid to skateboard. He jumped at the opportunity.

The eyes of the skateboarding world were now on Tony. Stacy Peralta, one of the sport's top stars, was as impressed as anyone. He asked Tony to join his team, the Bones Brigade. Tony didn't hesitate. This was a chance to compete with the best.

Tough Start

Tony entered his first skateboarding contest when he was 11. It was a real learning experience. He tossed and turned in bed the night before the competition. Then he froze when it came time to skate. He couldn't do anything right, and it showed in the marks the judges gave him. Hawk still doesn't know his final scores from that day. He asked his parents to drive him home before he received them. He later realized that being calm and focused in competition is crucial to becoming a champion.

Captured on Film

Joining the Bones Brigade also gave Tony the opportunity to become a "movie star." Peralta filmed videos of his riders. Tony was featured in many of them. The Bones Brigade videos were very popular with skateboarders and helped promote the sport.

Fast Fact

Stacy Peralta wrote and directed an award-winning movie about the early days of skateboarding called *Dogtown and Z-Boys*.

66His mind tells him he can do things his body can't do.99

–Nancy Hawk, on her son Tony

Trial and Error

Tony has no specific formula for inventing new tricks. "Sometimes I have an idea and go out to the skate park to try it out," he says. "It may not work, or I look at the ramp and don't even want to try it. But other times, I try something and then, wow! A new trick!" Tony's trial-and-error system has helped him invent more tricks than any other skateboarder.

Boys of Summer

Tony spent the summer of 1981 traveling the United States with the Bones Brigade. They competed in cities on both coasts. Life was exciting for Tony, but not always easy. Just barely a teenager, he missed his family, and the competition was fierce.

Tony knew, however, that he was gaining important experience that would pay off for years to come. He was surrounded by professionals such as Rodney Mullen, Steve Caballero, and Mike McGill. Tony learned something new about skateboarding every day.

On the Move

When Tony returned from his summer tour, his parents told him that the family was moving. The Hawks were heading north to Cardiff, a town in California about 20 miles (32 kilometers) north of San Diego.

Tony was excited for the change. Oasis skate park had become run-down. It was no longer a good place for Tony to practice. He was eager to find a new skate park. He also looked forward to starting at a new school. He hoped to make friends who were as crazy about skateboarding as he was.

Steve Caballero, a member of the Bones Brigade who taught Tony a lot about skateboarding.

CHAPTER 3

Family Matters

For many kids, their teenage years are an awkward time. Their bodies change, and they are unsure of themselves. They don't feel as if they fit in. Life can seem confusing and scary.

Tony knows this as well as anyone. By his teenage years, skateboarding had become an important part of his life. Many kids, however, still didn't think the sport was "cool." That made Tony an **outcast**. He was thankful to have a loving family that supported him and helped him through tough times.

School Daze

Tony entered San Dieguito Union High School in Encinitas, California, as a freshman in the fall of 1981. He was excited for a fresh start, but for him school was anything but fun. Older students teased him all the time. They didn't like skateboarding and picked on kids who did.

Tony strikes a serious pose for a high school yearbook photo.

The members of the school board were opposed to the sport, too. They believed it was dangerous and encouraged rowdy behavior.

Tony was crushed when San Dieguito banned skateboarding. He cheered up after finding a great skate park called the Del Mar Surf and Turf. That park became Tony's home away from home.

Fast Fact

One of Tony's most famous tricks is the stalefish. He credits a Swedish fan with naming it.

Super Sophomore

After Tony's rough freshman year at San Dieguito, his parents decided to send him to a new school. Tony loved Torrey Pines High School. In fact, the principal was a big fan of skateboarding.

Meanwhile, Tony's father, Frank, began exploring new ways to increase skateboarding's popularity. He started a new league called the National Skateboarding Association (NSA). For the first time, skaters across the country had a chance to compete against each other.

Tony won the first NSA championship, in 1982. Some skaters complained that he had an advantage because his dad ran the organization. Everyone agreed, however, that the NSA was good for skateboarding. It was helping the sport reach new fans and become more popular.

Fast Fact

Hawk is not the only famous graduate of Torrey Pines. Snowboarding superstar Shaun White also attended the school.

66 He could never leave a park until he perfected a trick. 99

—Steve Hawk, talking about his brother, Tony

Tony poses for a photo in 1983. He toured with the Bones Brigade that summer.

Summer Fun

During the summer of 1983, Tony took a break from the NSA and toured again with the Bones Brigade. This time, he traveled to Australia, Europe, and Canada. It was a chance for him to make a name for himself outside of the United States and see parts of the world he had never visited.

During this time, Tony also won a competition in St. Petersburg, Florida. It was his first victory outside of California. Skateboarding fans marveled at Tony wherever he went.

A Real Scare

By Tony's junior year at Torrey Pines, he was happier than ever. School was great. He had lots of friends, and his grades were good. Skateboarding was even better. In the fall of 1984, he won his second NSA championship. Tony also appeared in a skateboarding video called the *Bones Brigade Video Show*. Skateboarding fans began to recognize him wherever he went.

Before the year ended, however, Tony had a terrible scare. His father suffered a heart attack. Tony was with him when it happened and he called 9-1-1 for medical help. Frank survived, and Tony appreciated more than ever how much his family meant to him.

On the Rise

Frank was soon back running the NSA. Tony, meanwhile, was taking skateboarding by storm. No one had ever seen a rider like Tony. He soared through the air with incredible ease and grace. No one could match his tricks.

Tony won his third NSA championship in 1985. The next year, he earned a part in a movie called *Thrashin'* that featured all sorts of cool skateboarding tricks. Next, he appeared in the movie *Gleaming the Cube*. He also starred in a commercial for Mountain Dew and did another video, *The Search for Animal Chin*.

Through skateboarding, Tony made enough money to buy his own house. And he was still just a teenager.

Fast Fact

In 1987, Tony was hired as the stunt double for the actor David Spade in *Police Academy 4*. He was let go after producers realized he was 1 foot (0.3 meter) taller than Spade.

❝ I never thought I could make a career out of skateboarding.❞

–Tony Hawk

Bumps and Bruises

Tony has had his fair share of injuries while skateboarding. He always wears protective gear, including a helmet, knee pads, and elbow pads. But wipeouts are part of the sport. In his most serious crash, he fractured his skull and hip bone. He has also broken an elbow and suffered a few head injuries called **concussions**. There is one fall that makes Tony smile. It knocked out his two front teeth. For a serious skateboarder like him, that's a badge of honor.

Ramping It Up

After graduating from high school in 1986, Tony Hawk focused on his career. He decided he needed a new home with enough property to create his own personal skate park. It would be the best way to work on his skateboarding technique. He found the perfect place in Fallbrook, California.

Hawk and his father then got down to business. They spent day and night building a huge ramp and half-pipe. When they were done, Hawk had the ultimate skateboarding training ground.

Wedding Bells

Skateboarding wasn't the only thing on Hawk's mind. While he was in high school, he met a girl named Cindy Dunbar. The two began dating. Cindy often traveled with Tony on his skateboarding tours.

In April 1990, Tony and Cindy got married. Hawk also gained new sponsors, such as Swatch and Hot Wheels. He wondered if life could get any better. Little did Hawk know that skateboarding was about to hit some tough times. And so was he.

Fast Friends

Tony Hawk met an amazing athlete named Shaun White when White was 9. They have been friends ever since. White has managed to make a name for himself in not one sport, but two. He's a champion skateboarder as well as an Olympic gold medal–winning snowboarder. White and Hawk share a passion for trying new tricks and pushing the limit.

Hawk and Shaun White go airborne.

CHAPTER 4

X-traordinary Events

No one can escape problems. Indeed, life is full of many different kinds of challenges. Some people shy away from them. Other people face them head-on.

Hawk falls into the second group. He has faced more than one test in his life. Each time, he has attacked the problem. That's actually one of his secrets as a skateboarder. When he falls off his board, he gets back up and tries again. He doesn't give up. Hawk does the same thing in life.

Hawk is one of his sport's top business minds. He launched Birdhouse Projects in 1994.

Fading Fast

In the early 1990s, Hawk worried about the future of skateboarding. The sport had enjoyed enormous popularity for nearly a decade. But passion for the sport had begun to fade. Companies that made skateboarding equipment and clothes were going out of business.

Meanwhile, some of Hawk's sponsors could no longer afford to pay him. The NSA had to cancel competitions because of money problems. Hawk no longer felt as if he was on the top of the world. In spite of this downturn, Hawk started his own company, Birdhouse Projects (which became Birdhouse Skateboards) in 1994.

Fast Fact

Before big competitions, Hawk likes to eat either a turkey sandwich or two cheeseburgers, fries, and a soda from McDonald's.

Good News, Bad News

In March 1992, Tony and Cindy Hawk had a child, a boy named Riley. Their marriage, however, was in bad shape. They argued often and had to sell the house in Fallbrook. In 1994, they decided to divorce.

Hawk was down in the dumps. Things got worse when he got distressing news from his father. Frank had cancer.

Hawk needed some good news. He got it from ESPN. The cable sports network was planning an Olympics for extreme athletes. It would be called the X Games. Hawk could barely wait to compete.

Like Father, Like Son

Riley Hawk followed in his father's footsteps. He began skating as early as age 10. Since then he's made a name for himself in the skateboarding world. Everyone seems to agree that he's inherited his dad's talent. But Riley has developed his own unique style.

Tony poses with his oldest son, Riley Hawk.

The X Games

The first X Games were held in San Diego, California, in June 1995. The event included two skateboarding competitions, the **vert** and the **street**. The vert involves competition on ramps and other vertical structures. Street competition is on curbs, rails, and other aspects of the street environment. Hawk flew to victory in the vert and finished second in the street. The X Games gave skateboarding a major boost.

Saying Good-bye

In the midst of the sport's rebirth, skateboarding lost one of its heroes. Frank Hawk died after the 1995 X Games. Tony and his family were heartbroken. Frank's funeral helped them deal with their grief. People from every corner of the skateboarding world showed up to honor Frank's memory.

"I never set a plan for my life. I just rolled with it."

–Tony Hawk

The Loop

One of skateboarding's most daring tricks is the loop. It's done on a special circular ramp. The rider must build up enough speed to make a complete loop. At the top of the ramp, the rider is actually speeding along upside down. Hawk tried the loop for the first time in 1995. It took him two years to complete the trick successfully. To this day, he says it's the scariest thing he's ever done on a skateboard.

In Honor of Dad

After Frank's death, Hawk took a closer look at his life. His first thoughts were to slow down and take it easy. Then he thought about his dad. Frank had instilled in his kids a strong work ethic. Hawk knew his dad would want him to get back on his board and work even harder.

Hawk felt energized. He hired his sister Patricia to run Birdhouse Projects. He also launched a nationwide tour to promote the company. Hawk jumped back into competition, winning events in Las Vegas and Texas. He skated at the 1996 X Games despite an ankle injury. He still managed a second-place finish in the vert singles.

Fast Fact

Hawk gave fans at the 1996 X Games a special thrill when he finished his final run with a skateboard leap into the Pacific Ocean.

I Do

As Hawk's career picked up, so did his personal life. After his divorce from Cindy, he began dating a woman named Erin Lee. Tony's son Riley was as crazy about Erin as he was. In 1996, Tony and Erin got married and went to Hawaii for their honeymoon.

All the while, new tricks were swirling inside Hawk's head. The most intriguing one was the 900. Was it really possible? Hawk had to find out.

Swing of Things

The Disney animated movie *Tarzan* opened in 1999. But the movie took years of work before it made it to theaters. One question that stumped animators was how to create the effect of Tarzan swinging from vine to vine in the jungle. Guess who was their inspiration? Tony Hawk, of course. Many of Tarzan's moves are re-creations of Hawk floating through the air on his skateboard. Hawk also did a commercial for the movie. For that, he built a special ramp and did many of his best tricks.

Hawk's skateboarding was the inspiration for some of Tarzan's moves.

CHAPTER 5

Going Out on a High Note

What makes professional athletes tick? They love competition. They love challenging themselves to get better. They love their sport.

Not surprisingly, it's hard for a professional athlete to know when to retire. Just ask Hawk. By the late 1990s, he had been skateboarding for nearly two decades. His body ached a little more after every fall. Many of his competitors were half his age. Could he imagine life without riding professionally? Maybe, but not until he pulled off the 900.

Practice Time

At the beginning of 1997, Hawk was hard at work on the 900. He tried it for the first time in competition at the X Games that year. With the crowd cheering him on, he gave the 900 a shot. Hawk wound up flat on his back! Thanks to his first two runs, however, he still took first place in the vert.

By 1997, completing the 900 was Hawk's main focus in skateboarding.

That wasn't the last time Hawk would take a tumble while attempting the 900. He spent plenty of time practicing the trick in 1998. In between, he produced his first video, *The End*. It became the top-selling video in skateboarding history. Hawk kept up his winning ways in competition, too. He won a total of nine titles that year.

Fast Fact

Hawk teamed with Andy Macdonald to win the first vert doubles competition at the 1997 X Games.

Decisions, Decisions

Hawk's life was busier than ever. In March 1999, Erin gave birth to a baby boy. They named him Spencer.

Hawk also took an important step in his career. With business offers coming in from every direction, he hired an **agent**. Some people criticized him. They thought he was "selling out" to sponsors that did not have the sport's best interests at heart. Hawk believed an agent would help him make skateboarding even more popular.

That year, Hawk also decided to retire from full-time competition. He wanted to spend more time with his family and work on his business. It was time to let the new generation of riders take center stage.

Looking Good, Doing Good

Hawk's line of clothes is one of skateboarding's best success stories. Today, the collection includes styles for young boys and teenagers, plus a large selection of shoes. Two years after Hawk launched Hawk Clothing, it was bought by a surfing company called Quicksilver. Then the Kohl's department store chain began selling the apparel. Hawk donates part of the profits from Hawk Clothing to charity. Some of that money goes to building new skate parks in Europe.

Tony performs his signature trick, the 900.

Mr. 900

Before the young athletes got their shot, however, Hawk took one more run at history. At the 1999 X Games, he finally landed the 900. The joy on his face afterward showed how much the trick meant to him.

Hawk was smiling again a few months later. In September 1999, the first version of his video game *Pro Skater* hit stores nationwide. It flew off the shelves. At the same time, Hawk's line of apparel, known as Hawk Clothing, was selling equally well.

Fast Fact

Hawk says the idea for the 900 first came to him when he was 19 years old.

Keeping Busy

Hawk was hotter than ever. He had always been popular with skateboarding fans. Now people who didn't follow the sport closely wanted to know more about him. So Hawk sat down with writer Sean Mortimer and wrote his **autobiography**. The book is called *Hawk: Occupation: Skateboarder*. The book was published in 2000 and sold millions of copies.

Hawk was feeling so good that he returned to the X Games that year. Fans across the country hoped he would do another 900. He didn't disappoint them. He pulled off the trick without a hitch.

Things got even busier in 2001, when the Hawks had another son. He was named Keegan.

Tony Hawk gives baby Keegan a ride.

Oh, Brother

Not everyone is a fan of Hawk's. Some people are jealous of his success. Others think he overshadows competitors who have unique talents of their own. In a poll once conducted by *Big Brother* magazine, Hawk was voted his sport's "most hated" skater. In the same poll, he also finished second for the sport's "most liked" skater.

Hawk takes time to sign autographs for his fans.

Ready For Anything

Hawk was back on top. Thanks to Hawk Clothing and *Pro Skater*, business was booming. After his second 900 at the X Games, he proved he could still thrill the fans on his skateboard.

Was there anything left for Hawk to tackle? Without a doubt! He remembered how his father had always been eager to find new challenges. Hawk was no different.

> **"**It's exciting to be upside down in the air and have the feeling I know where I'm at.**"**
>
> –Tony Hawk

CHAPTER 6

Flying High

No matter what the sport, it seems that fans love a good debate. There's one question that never fails to start an argument in any sport: Who's the best ever?

Skateboarding fans can spend hours on that topic. Of course, they usually arrive at the same answer: Tony Hawk. Even after he stopped competing, Hawk found ways to be a leader in his sport. One thing is certain: skateboarding would not be the same without him.

Big Bang

Hawk's quest to grow the sport of skateboarding was endless. In 2002, he came up with an exciting new idea. Hawk thought it would be fun to combine skateboarding with other extreme sports in one massive show. The Boom Boom Huck Jam was born.

Hawk performs in Las Vegas as part of his 2002 Boom Boom Huck Jam tour.

The first show was held in Las Vegas in 2002. It featured skateboarders, BMX riders, and freestyle moto-x performers. Hawk also recruited rocking music acts. Boom Boom Huck Jam was a smash hit. Before long, Hawk took the show on the road. Today, the tour stops in more than 30 cities across the United States. It sells out almost everywhere it goes.

Fast Fact

In 2005, the Boom Boom Huck Jam did a special show at the Super Bowl.

Reaching Out

Hawk proved he was as good a businessman as he was a skateboarder. He also thought about all the people in the world less fortunate than he was. He wanted to reach out to them, but how?

In 2002, he started the Tony Hawk Foundation. Skateboarding had rescued Hawk from bullies, bad grades, and other struggles when he was a kid. He hoped the sport could do the same for others. That was his motivation for starting the foundation. Through skateboarding, he would teach children to live productive, healthy lives. As of 2008, the foundation had raised more than $2 million and built skate parks throughout the United States.

Tony Hawk appears in the 300th episode of The *Simpsons* TV show.

Tony and Lhotse Hawk pose for a photo with their daughter, Kadence.

Starting Over

By 2004, everything in Hawk's life was good, except for his marriage. He and Erin divorced that year. Hawk was sad to see his marriage end. He spent more time with his sons to help them adjust.

Supporting his sons also made it easier for Hawk to deal with the disappointment of his divorce. Soon, he began dating a woman named Lhotse Merriam. The two were married in 2006.

Two years later, they welcomed a baby girl to the family. Tony and Lhotse named her Kadence.

Fast Fact

The rock band Rancid played at Tony and Lhotse's wedding.

What a Ride!

Meanwhile, the Boom Boom Huck Jam was the most popular skateboard tour in the United States. It drew its biggest crowds at Six Flags amusement parks.

That led to a new opportunity for Hawk. Six Flags created a roller coaster called Tony Hawk's Big Spin. It opened in St. Louis, Missouri, in 2007. A short time later, a second ride was added in San Antonio, Texas. In 2008, Six Flags in Washington, D.C., opened a water ride inspired by Hawk.

Also in 2008, Hawk started his own movie company—900 Films. His goal is to make movies that give fans new ways of looking at skateboarding.

Musician Jon Bon Jovi and Hawk take part in a skate park fund-raiser in 2008.

Reason For Hope

In 2007, Hawk teamed up with other stars in Athletes for Hope. The organization supports local charities worldwide. It also connects professional athletes with businesses and individuals who want to help.

Among the other big names that work with Athletes for Hope are Lance Armstrong, Mia Hamm, Andre Agassi, and Muhammad Ali.

NFL player Warrick Dunn and Hawk speak at an Athletes for Hope press conference.

Long Live the Birdman

Skateboarding has come a long way since Hawk took his first ride back in the 1970s. Millions of people enjoy the sport in countries all around the world. There are countless skateboarding web sites and numerous skateboarding magazines.

In other words, skateboarding has gone mainstream. Could this have happened without Tony Hawk? No one knows for sure. But it's clear that the sport has spread its wings and soared to new heights, thanks to the Birdman.

Time Line

1968 Tony Hawk is born on May 12 in San Diego, California.

1977 Hawk gets his first skateboard.

1982 Hawk wins his first NSA title.

1986 Hawk appears in the movie *Thrashin'*.

1994 Hawk starts Birdhouse Projects.

1999 Hawk lands the 900 at the X Games.

2002 The Tony Hawk Foundation is created.

2007 Tony Hawk's Big Spin debuts at Six Flags in St. Louis, Missouri.

2008 Hawk starts his own movie company, 900 Films.

Glossary

adrenaline: a substance produced by the body during times of great excitement. It provides more energy and strength.

agent: a person who represents someone else in business dealings

autobiography: a book written by someone about his or her own life

concussions: injuries to the brain caused by a heavy blow to the head. Concussions can result in unconsciousness, dizziness, or sickness.

half-pipe: a skateboarding ramp that looks like a round pipe cut into a semicircle

outcast: someone who is ignored or shunned by others

900: a move that requires two and half turns in midair

ramp: a skateboarding device used by a rider to go faster. Each side of a half-pipe is a ramp.

rebels: people who don't follow the rules of a society

street: a type of skateboarding competition that involves moves on curbs, rails, and other aspects of the street environment

vert: a type of skateboarding competition that involves moves on ramps and other vertical structures

Find Out More

Books

Cobb, Allan. B. *Skating the X Games* (Super Skateboarding). New York: Rosen Central, 2009.

Hawk, Tony, and Sean Mortimer. *Hawk: Occupation: Skateboarder.* New York: Regan Books, 2000.

Hawk, Tony, and Sean Mortimer. *Stalefish: Skateboard Culture From the Rejects Who Made It.* New York: Chronicle Books, 2008.

Kennedy, Mike. *Shaun White* (Today's Superstars). Pleasantville, NY: Gareth Stevens Publishing, 2010.

Web Sites

Tony Hawk's Official Web Site
www.tonyhawk.com
Learn more about Tony Hawk's life and accompishments.

Tony Hawk Foundation
www.tonyhawkfoundation.org/
Get the latest news about Hawk's charitable work.

Tony Hawk's Boom Boom Huck Jam
www.boomboomhuckjam.com
Check out Tony Hawk's skateboarding show.

Publisher's note to educators and parents: Our editors have carefully reviewed these web sites to ensure that they are suitable for children. Many web sites change frequently, however, and we cannot guarantee that a site's future contents will continue to meet our high standards of quality and educational value. Be advised that children should be closely supervised whenever they access the Internet.

Source Notes

p. 6: "Hawk Shows Off, Makes Skateboarding History," ESPN press release, June 27, 1999.

p. 7: "Tony Hawk...flies like an eagle," AskMen.com, www.askmen.com/celebs/interview/28_tony_hawk_interview.html.

p. 12: Sean Mortimer, "Chairman of the Board," *Sports Illustrated for Kids*, 1998.

p. 15: Tony Hawk's official web site, TonyHawk.com, 2009.

p. 20: Armen Keteyian, "Chairman of the Board," *Sports Illustrated*, November 24, 1986.

p. 23: TonyHawk.com, 2009.

p. 29: Mortimer, "Chairman of the Board."

p. 37: Sean Mortimer, "Chairman of the Board."

Index

About the Author

Mike Kennedy is a huge sports fan who has written dozens of books for kids, including one called *Skateboarding*. Mike grew up in Ridgewood, New Jersey, and went to Franklin & Marshall College, where he earned letters in baseball and football. Today, Mike loves to run on trails and play golf. He and his wife, Ali, live in Boulder, Colorado.

WALKING
ONE ANOTHER HOME

Moments of Grace and Possibility
in the Midst of Alzheimer's

RITA BRESNAHAN

Liguori/Triumph
LIGUORI, MISSOURI

Imprimi Potest:
Richard Thibodeau, C.Ss.R.
Provincial, Denver Province
The Redemptorists

Published by Liguori/Triumph
An imprint of Liguori Publications
Liguori, Missouri
www.liguori.org
www.catholicbooksonline.com

Quote from "Four Quartets" by T. S. Eliot, copyright 1943, 1971, A Harvest Book, Harcourt, Brace & World, Inc., New York, is used with permission of publisher.

Library of Congress Cataloging-in-Publication Data

Bresnahan, Rita.
    Walking one another home : moments of grace and possibility in the midst of Alzheimer's / Rita Bresnahan. 1st ed.
        p.   cm.
    Includes bibliographical references.
    ISBN 0-7648-0936-9
    1. Alzheimer's disease—Patients—Home care. 2. Alzheimer's disease—Patients—Family relationships. 3. Mothers—Mental health. 4. Caregivers. I. Title.

RC523.2.B74 2003
362.1'96831—dc21   2002043287

Printed in the United States of America
07 06 05 04 03   5 4 3 2 1
First edition

DEDICATION

I dedicate this book
to my mother and father—
who taught me to walk gently
and to live simply on this earth;
to know what true riches are;
to appreciate what I have.
Their faith and love,
their lives and their stories,
gave me mine.

CONTENTS

ACKNOWLEDGMENTS

∽∾

I hereby declare that it takes a village to raise an author. It really does.

For launching this project, I am grateful to the staff at Liguori Publications, particularly Judy Bauer, managing editor. Her perseverance and her confidence in my writing guided me through this first publishing experience. Thanks also to literary agent Tom Grady, who understood my perspective and vision from the beginning. I cannot overemphasize the value of his observations and constructive criticism.

I owe a special indebtedness to Mary Smoluch, my Northwest editor-sister. Her critic's eye—tough, insightful, and candid—reviewed every page of nearly every draft. Her keen editing skills—organizing, rearranging, time sequencing—were critical in weaving so many pieces into the "big picture." To Bev Forbes, Kathy Fischer, and Ramona Adams, I offer my heartfelt thanks for their unflagging support and wise literary critique; indeed, they helped mid-wife various drafts of the manuscript.

Readers Marty Richards and Richard Gordon were also generous with feedback from their hearts, minds, and spiritual perspectives.

I thank my extensive team of computer experts who launched me, kicking and screaming, into the cyberspace world—and helped ground me back on planet Earth when I got lost out there. Without them I'd still be pecking away on a Royal.

I owe a special thanks to Deb Dollard for her generous open-ended invitation to use Rainbow End as nurturing writing haven. There at the water, much of this writing came into being.

Finally, my heart is full of gratitude for the enduring love, support, and good humor of my brothers and sisters—Patti, Dick, Jerry, and Mary. How blessed I feel to be part of the Bresnahan family.

In the wider world I am beholden to a network of good friends and colleagues larger than I could ever thank by name.

So, thanks to all of you in my village. I am grateful to each one for walking with me on this journey.

INTRODUCTION

Alzheimer's. The very word sends shivers up and down the American spine. Four million families in the United States are affected; one in ten has a relative with this disease. Indeed, few experiences have touched me as profoundly as my mother's struggle with Alzheimer's. When she was diagnosed in 1989, the literature dealt primarily with practical aspects: legal, financial, nursing-care needs, and the like. Not being responsible for those matters, I was concerned about more personal, soul-searching questions. I began journaling, exploring them.

The early 1990s were filled with a growing concern about Alzheimer's. Countless adult children faced the dilemma of how to be loving and supportive to ailing parents while living at a distance. A flourishing interest in spirituality was also emerging. I did not realize at the time of my visits with Mom that my journaling would provide material for stories I would later write. But as *Walking One Another Home* evolved, I dis-

covered these nineties themes to be prominent throughout
my writing as well.

Composed of stories woven together over the course of
witnessing my mother struggle with Alzheimer's, this book is
about mothers and daughters, about caregivers and the gifts
arising out of caregiving. The stories also reflect how my thirty
years as a psychotherapist, educator, and spiritual counselor
challenged me to make this stressful journey into an enlight-
ening one. To become a better person in the process. To deal
with anger, guilt, and harsh judgments. To accept my own
failings....To help me understand myself more fully as well as
my mother. I faced great anguish and joy in the process, so I
include in the stories some creative ways I found of approaching delicate situations.

Although I was not my mother's primary caregiver, it was
important to stay connected, involved in her life. Living fifteen
hundred miles away, I had to make the best out of extended
visits to the nursing home. I thought it might be helpful for
those of you in similar situations if I shared what I learned
over the years. My professional training certainly provided a
repertoire of strategies to draw upon. Spiritual practices also
enlightened and softened these times, reminding me time and
again to be faithful to the path with heart. I tried to shape
each visit into the most positive experience possible, to de-
velop certain virtues which fostered a gentle way of being. To
focus simply on whatever was at hand.

These were not easy tasks, but I vowed to stretch and

deepen parts of myself even in the midst of such heartache as Alzheimer's. The book challenges stereotypes about the disease, shifting the emphasis away from fear and horror, to love and possibility. It explores ways to enrich a relationship by responding to the movement of grace during visits—ways such as remembering what really matters, staying in the present, being aware, compassionate, playful. It serves as a reminder to count our blessings and appreciate what we have, to be generous in sharing with others, to know what true riches are, to laugh at life's surprises, to live gracefully in the Spirit.

This book then is about much more than Alzheimer's. It speaks to countless situations where a person feels helpless in the face of loss or other challenging circumstances. It is about loving, intentional, and spirited ways of living, especially in difficult times. For then such a simple act as making popcorn becomes an awakening, the unexpected becomes an everyday expectation, the sick one becomes the teacher, and the most upsetting circumstances become spiritual opportunities.

The wonder of it all: that each of us reading this, each day, gets to choose the meaning we place on the events of our lives, gets to choose how to perceive them, how to translate them into our own healing. As I look back, I realize that my mother's illness touched me in most unfathomable ways, calling me to an awareness of the sacred that will abide with me all of my days. How deeply I have been changed by this pilgrimage....

I realize that everyone's "walk" is different. My hope is

that some stories in the following pages remind you to search for the sacred in your own everyday relationships. To draw upon some inner strength in dealing with a loved one's loss of physical or mental capacities. Perhaps in these pages you can find fresh ways of responding that offer solutions for your own journey, practical ways of easing time spent together, ways of meeting a loved one and yourself a bit more fully, a bit more gently.

So I tell my stories. I trust them to touch those of you who have relatives, friends, or loved ones suffering from Alzheimer's, to help you feel not quite so alone. I trust parts of them to tell your story as well. To help you recognize and respond to the moments of grace and possibility that present themselves every day in your own life.

I thank you for walking with me through these pages. I believe that's why we are here on this earth: to walk one another home.

Blessings on your journey....

PRELUDE

O h! Look at those flowers! Aren't they beautiful?"
Mom ooh's and ahhhh's as we step into her nursing-
home room after lunch.

It's as if they arrived at this very moment. It's as if she has
never seen them before, although this is the second day the
bouquet has graced her dresser. She has been surprised by the
flowers, admiring their beauty anew each time she has caught
sight of them.

"Did you get them for me?"

"I did, Mom. I know how much you like summery bou-
quets."

"Why, thank you," she says.

Always "thank you." It's amazing how the forgetfulness
that can be so frustrating in Alzheimer's can also at times like
today turn into delight.

This day this gift keeps on giving...and giving...

Such unconditional appreciation and gratefulness of spirit were always alive in my mother. Born in East St. Louis, Illinois, in 1905, Miriam Rita Vermeersch was the fifth of eight children. On her father's side, she was Belgian; on her mother's, French-Canadian and American Indian. (Cherokee? I'm not certain. Her mother always guarded that secret very carefully.) In 1931, Miriam married Farley Bresnahan, a smiling Irishman with a relentless sense of humor. Both were devout Catholics, and their faith formed the bedrock of our family life. Together they had three sons—Dick, Bob, and Jerry; and three daughters—Mary, Patti, and myself. In 1934, Dad's railroad job moved us to Pekin, Illinois, to a home only a hundred yards from the lake in Mineral Springs Park. We all grew up there, claiming the park and the lake as our own.

Miriam was a devoted mother who literally worked night and day raising six kids. She cooked delicious meals on a limited income, and made unforgettable cherry pie. Mom hummed as she ironed or hung laundry for her growing family, sang along with records of Mario Lanza, played by ear lots of tunes on the piano, and crooned lullabies to the newest baby.

My dad died in 1959 at the young age of fifty-four, leaving Mom with three teenagers to raise. For months Mom cried herself to sleep at night; in fact, she never quite fully recovered from that loss. She refused to return to the social stream, and for years, she even stopped singing. Although her faith was shaken for a while, she continued attending Mass every day and praying the rosary every night.

Mom immediately found a job as a receptionist for a doctor's office, and her ability to work with people began to blossom. Then, after her youngest children were launched, she began volunteering for various causes: in the Share program; at the Blood Bank; with St. Vincent de Paul services for the poor; as a minister who brought the Eucharist to residents of two nearby nursing homes. In her early eighties, Mom was still picking up friends to go grocery shopping or to Mass. She managed on her own for thirty-five years after Dad died, until she could no longer safely live alone.

My brother Dick lives in the Quad-Cities, where Illinois and Iowa touch at the Mississippi River. We encouraged Mom to consider moving there. Dick could then keep us all current about Mom's state of well-being.

The rest of us are scattered around the country, with Jerry in Los Angeles, Mary in Eugene, Oregon, and Patti in Brainerd, Minnesota. Our brother Bob, the only one of us to continue living in Pekin close to Mom, died of leukemia in 1988 at the age of fifty-one. I live in Seattle, Washington, fifteen hundred miles from Mom. I do not classify myself as a "caregiver" in the most traditional sense. I am simply a caring daughter who would like to live closer to her mother, and who deeply longs for the time she does share with her mother to be meaningful and memorable.

Shortly after Mom was diagnosed with Alzheimer's disease, when she was in her late eighties, I spent a summer back in the Midwest to have extended time with her while she was adjusting to her first year of nursing-home living. Although she was struggling with moderate symptoms of Alzheimer's, there was still a fairly intact Miriam to whom others could relate. It was an intensely frustrating time for her, however, as she became keenly aware that she was losing herself and her capacities. I spent long, leisurely days with Mom, without time constraints, to comfort both of us. Only in retrospect did I truly see the sacredness of that time together.

My commitment for that summer was to pray, meditate, read, and journal for a few hours each morning, then have lunch with Mom and spend the remainder of the day being together. After dusk, I would return to St. Mary's Convent in Moline, Illinois, about ten minutes from my mother, and write again for another hour or two. I did not realize at the time that this journaling would provide material for the stories I would later write. As the writing emerged, however, I was surprised to find that it was not so much about Mom's Alzheimer's as it was about my own spirit travels into and around that world, my own inner pilgrimage of love and faith. T. S. Eliot's words kept coming to me:

> *And what you thought you came for*
> *Is only a shell, a husk of meaning*
> *From which the purpose breaks only when it is fulfilled.*
> *If at all.*

PART I

THE CALLING

Miriam Bresnahan
at her high-school
graduation.

Miriam Bresnahan
stylishly attired
sometime in the
1920s.

What was curious to me, at the onset of Mom's disease, was that I, too, felt disoriented. Although I had read volumes on Alzheimer's, I could find no clear road map, no specific time frame to mark the passages. Yes, research literature does describe stages and sequences, but it offers no clear definitions. What's more, I find each stage and sequence to be quite subjective, as each person is so different in unique and unpredictable ways.

In my disoriented state, I began pondering—which is almost a way of life for me. Ever since I was a teenager, I have been an avid student of any subject that sheds light on how we create meaning throughout this life of ours. How are we to respond to life's deep questions such as "Who am I?" "Why am I here?" "Where am I going?" "How do I get there?" "Where am I now?" Through the years, I have pored over hundreds of books on psychology, religion, philosophy, mythology, and ritual, all of which have left impressions on my soul. It is only natural, then, at this soul-searching time, that I should insist on asking myself, *So, if there is no clear road map out there, Rita, how will you find "your" way as companion through the Alzheimer journey?* It's also only natural that I should reflect on which rich insights and familiar treasured sources might provide a sketchy map for me, might guide me, might offer me fresh perspective and meaning. The words of Spanish poet Antonio Machado's were both unsettling and reassuring: "Traveler, there is no path. Paths are made by walking."

I found inspiration from many sources, but one book spoke

to me most deeply: *The Art of Pilgrimage: A Seeker's Guide to Making Travel Sacred* by Phil Cousineau (Conari Press, 1998). His wise words, "We can transform any journey into pilgrimage with a commitment to finding something personally sacred along the road," resonated with how my own journey was unfolding. Only as I opened to the sacredness of this image did I begin to understand the uniqueness and the depth of such a pilgrimage through Alzheimer's. When I did make the commitment to find something sacred along the road each day, my heart began responding in new ways to my mother's Alzheimer's and to my own spiritual life. My writing soon began to bring together these two unlikely companions—Alzheimer's and spirituality—through the metaphor of a pilgrimage.

Pilgrims leave their comfortable everyday surroundings to venture, at least for a while, into challenging and unfamiliar territory. Often they journey to places where a holy presence is felt, places credited with healing powers.

Consistently, I felt a holy presence when I was with my mother, and her tiny nursing-home room offered healing at many levels. True, absurd dilemmas often arose, stirring strange and unwelcome feelings in me. At such times, I would become impatient or preoccupied or even depressed as I witnessed Mom's downward spiral. Watching someone I love so much fade before my very eyes was not easy, and often made me feel helpless. What could I do? Being helpless seemed pretty much a given in this situation. I myself needed help—help from a power far beyond my own. Help tempering my testy and challenging times.

But this much is clear: I cannot do anything about Mom's deteriorating condition. What I could do something about was my own behavior. I could bring into our interactions greater love and compassion, more patience and flexibility. In each given moment, this is my call....

I am not helpless after all....

Yes, we walked one another home faithfully, Mom and I, in our pilgrimage through Alzheimer's. In tender and sacred times...through the darkness and the light...step by step.

Through each story.

Each encounter.

Through each day.

Each moment.

> *"Life is so full of meaning and purpose,*
> *so full of beauty—*
> *beneath its covering...*
>
> *Courage, then, to claim it...*
> *and the knowledge that we are pilgrims together,*
> *wending our way*
> *through unknown country, home."*
> FRA GIOVANNI

Chapter One

SIGNS ON THE HORIZON

The first task of my pilgrimage required that I learn to read certain signs as they appeared on the horizon. What called me at this particular time came from signs indicating the steady deterioration of my mother's condition. These signs beckoned me to join her in a pilgrimage through Alzheimer's that would ultimately lead us both "home"—to the home that poet John Cage reminds us is ours: "We carry our home within us, which enables us to fly." Home, where we can be our truest Self, where we feel connected, safe, and "at home" in the deepest sense.

The three stories that follow span six years and depict my mother's beginning stages of Alzheimer's. Nearly two years elapse between each of them. They represent three major transitions for Mom and for our entire family.

"Wake Up, Sleepyhead" describes the stunning realization

that Mom's mental capacity is markedly diminishing. Although we (her "kids") are uneasy with the turn of events, we do not feel immediate, radical action is needed. Although Mom has been quite skilled at masking her symptoms, we now are on high alert.

Interestingly, Mom's words offer meaning for me beyond what she intended, for "waking up"—becoming aware, staying in the present moment—is the very heart and soul of pilgrimage. And as I was to ruefully discover, it is not a case of waking up once and for all, but a moment-by-moment calling.

At the time the story "Walking One Another Home" takes place, Mom is eighty-eight years old and the family can no longer deny the seriousness of her condition. Once we realize that she cannot safely manage to live in her own home, we know the decision we must make. We so want to spare Mom the pain of this move, of leaving behind everything familiar. Would that we could make everything all right again, but of course we cannot hold back the darkness. Suddenly we realize that this is a passage for each of us as well: our mother is leaving the only house we ever called "home" in all our growing-up years.

"I'll Never Love You Again" recounts the dreaded and heart-wrenching move to a nursing home that ensues two years later. We struggle with an increasingly fiercer honesty to accept the fact that Mom cannot care for herself in any way. Our mother's physical and mental abilities are deteriorating to the point of no return.

At first we use the term *dementia.*

Finally, *Alzheimer's.*

Wake Up, Sleepyhead

When I was a young girl, my mother always ushered in my birthday by shaking my shoulder gently and calling, "Wake up, Sleepyhead. It's your birthday!"

In my adult years, in spite of the fifteen hundred miles separating us, that tradition has continued. Like clockwork, the phone rings around 6 A.M. (8 A.M. her time) each year on November 9, and Mom's voice bugles her familiar reveille, "Wake up, Sleepyhead. It's your birthday! I wanted to catch you before you head off to work!" And then she sings "Happy Birthday" to me. I've never imagined my birthday starting any other way.

On my fifty-seventh birthday, however, there is no morning call. Not at 6 A.M. Not at 7 A.M. Not at 8 A.M. I leave the house reluctantly, telling myself there will be a message waiting for me when I return. But no, this evening there is nothing, not even the faithful birthday card in the mail, "With Love to My Daughter on Your Birthday." *Maybe tomorrow*, I assure myself.

Three long days pass, and still no word from Mom. Something *must* be wrong.

I decide to call my brother. Surely he will know. He lives

only an hour from Mom, and visits her frequently. When he answers the phone, I can barely speak. "Dick! I did not hear from Mom...on my birthday. Is she all right?"

There is a long silence on the other end. Then, taking a deep breath, my brother tells me softly, "Rita, Mom is just too confused about time and everything. One date is the same as another. Besides, she just cannot dial all of those numbers."

I am shocked. "Dick, I just spent ten days with Mom in August. True, she was becoming forgetful at that time, and repeated herself a lot, but 'one date is the same as the next?' That is serious!"

"Well it is, Rita. It's happening so fast. And I hate to tell you, but you won't get a card or anything from Mom again— unless I buy it for her at the appropriate time and send it." Each of us is careful not to speak aloud the dreaded word "Alzheimer's." But we both know.

Hanging up the phone, I burst out crying. I will not be getting any more calls or cards from Mom? For two more days I continue to be on the edge of tears, unable to reconcile the facts, uncertain about how to get on with my new year without Mom's greetings. What can I do?

Then it comes to me: I will call her and see if just speaking with her can bring me some semblance of peace.

"Oh hi, Rita," she says cheerily when she hears my voice. "What've you been up to?" She always asks that question.

I mention a few activities. Then hesitantly, "And I've been celebrating my birthday all week."

"Oh," she gasps, "did I remember to send you a card?"

Inspiration comes in the moment: "Well, Mom, that's why I'm calling. This year I would like a *singing* birthday card from you."

"A what?"

"A *singing* birthday card. I'd like you to *sing* 'Happy Birthday' to me instead of sending a card."

"Oh! Okay!" And without hesitating, she begins belting out the familiar tune:

> *"Happy Birthday to you,*
> *Happy Birthday to you,*
> *Happy Birthday my firstest girl-baby Rita,*
> *Happy Birthday to you!"*

And then she sings it through lustily a second time. I am laughing through my tears.

Before we hang up, I tell her, "Thanks for the singing birthday card, Mom. That's the best card I've ever received."

"It is?" she asks incredulously. "Well, then, I will send you one just like it *every* year."

She has kept her word.

Walking One Another Home

"If we let Mom stay alone in the house any longer, it will be neglect."

My brother's phone call sets in motion an immediate sequence of events. We must help our mother move from her home in Pekin, Illinois, where she has lived for nearly sixty years, into a retirement apartment a hundred miles away in Moline, where the eldest of her children lives, her priest-son, Dick. Knowing she will be close to him and able to attend his Mass every day somewhat softens Mom's heart to this agonizing move. Nevertheless, she is grief-stricken, angry, and completely overwhelmed.

In my mind's eye, I see Mom standing helplessly in the familiar yellow kitchen, shoulders drooped, sensing something "bad" is about to happen, not always remembering what. I cannot bear the thought of her there seven long days—alone— facing this heart-wrenching move from her precious roots.

The next day, I teach my classes in Seattle and then catch a red-eye special "home."

The seven days that follow are bittersweet: some of the richest of my life, challenging and poignant as well. Mom's confused state of mind is immediately apparent. For example, on the phone she had told me she'd begun to pack, but when I arrive, only two cardboard boxes stand open in the back bedroom. The bottom of one is graced by two tiny lace doilies she crocheted before she and Dad got married. The other box contains three rolls of toilet paper—nothing more. This is the extent of her "packing."

"I just don't know where to start, Rita." Already my heart is weeping with her.

Well, we do not start with packing. In fact, the whole week I am with her, we do not take down a single picture or upset the orderliness of the house in any way. No dismantling of her home yet. (My sisters' orders: "You be the advance team, Rita. Just be with her in the grieving and in the good-byes. When *we* get there, a week later, we will pack. Okay?" Okay. That's fine with me.)

So I wonder what might lift Mom's spirits. Maybe we can walk a bit by the lake. That is sure to do it. Some of my earliest and sharpest memories of my mother are of her walking. Everywhere, for the family owned no car. And what a confident, joyful walker she was! One remarkably vivid picture is engraved on my eleven-year-old memory: It is a hot August day. Mom is striding briskly along the lake across from our house— toward the hospital on the other side—on her way to give birth to my sister Mary. On the way to give birth! Striding! Briskly! Yes. Dad could scarcely keep up with her.

In a way, walking has always been a prime measure of Mom's state of well-being. Walking helps create a positive sense of herself, gives her a feeling of aliveness, of vitality. Walking is her medium, and mine too.

Walking around the lake across from our house became a daily treat for Mom in her later years, when all her kids were

grown, and once she has a car and doesn't have to walk everywhere else. It's also a favorite ritual of ours when I come to
visit. In the past three or four years, however, with her feet
swollen and aching, Mom has not been up to walking, much
to her great dismay—and mine. Nevertheless, before setting
off myself, I would always ask anyway, "Are you able to go
walking today, Mom?"

On my first day back during this tender week, I ask the
usual: "Are you able to go walking today, Mom?" Much to my
surprise—as if she has been waiting—she answers, "I sure am!"

Now it's about a half-mile walk around the lake—and we
traipse it three times, without a rest, pausing at each com-
pleted round to see if it's time to head home.

"Let's keep going!" Mom grins. ("See, I can still do this!")
We are both amazed and delighted at her newfound stamina.
And she is very proud.

In the next few days, however, Mom can scarcely walk at
all, certainly not around the lake; even getting in and out of
the car becomes a strain. "I must have overdone it that first
day, Rita."

Mom and I laugh a lot, cry a little, those seven days. We
keep life pretty normal. Most mornings we get up early and
drive to church for Mass. Sometimes we invite favorite cronies out to lunch. At any time of the day or night, we find
ourselves plunked down in the easy chairs in the living room,
just gazing for hours at our favorite sight: the lake and the
trees across from our house. How she loves that lake! We all

do. We watch some television—the news, especially the weather, *Lawrence Welk, Wheel of Fortune*. Each day the magic hour of five o'clock ushers in our traditional "Bresnahan happy hour." At 4:55 P.M., Mom begins arranging hors d'oeuvres while I fix drinks. Clinking our glasses in a toast signals "happy hour" has officially begun. (More than once that week, words for the toast stick in my throat.) After happy hour, we fix dinner together. Pop popcorn later. Maybe play some pinochle. All the while, a cloud hangs over these common ordinary things we have enjoyed through the years.

Mom's mini-strokes some weeks before have left her unable to drive, so we run errands she's not been able to do alone—go to the bank, to the grocery store, to K-Mart for Efferdent and other supplies. I drive her to get her hair permed—for the last time—by the beautician who has done it for thirty-five years. And we get her taxes figured by the same accountant who has performed that task for the Bresnahans since the early 1930s.

Back at the house, we find ourselves sitting and looking at that lake again, sometimes quietly, at other times reminiscing. Certain aspects of the lake always intrigue Mom.

"See how the water glistens, just like diamonds."

"The waves are really high today, aren't they, Rita?"

"Isn't the fountain pretty?"

"Look at all the people walking today. See that one in the funny red hat?"

Too soon, our time together comes to an end. It is my last

day home, the last one I will ever spend in this beloved house. I rise early so I can get some exercise before leaving for the airport. Mom, still in bed, calls out to me as she hears me tiptoe down the creaky stairs. I go into her room and sit at the edge of her bed for a moment. She sees I have my Nikes on. "Goin' walking?"

"Yeah, Mom, I am." Each day I've been home, I have invited her to join me, just in case. Except for that first day, both of us have been disappointed that she has been unable to take even a leisurely stroll. Maybe this morning she can. I sure hope so. "Are you up for a little walk with me at all, Mom?"

I hear the catch in her voice, "No...No, honey. My legs are hurting me too much. You go ahead." She looks so frail in her bed.

My heart is heavy as I step out into the chilly air—a foggy Illinois morning, with visibility perhaps a hundred yards. Setting off briskly, I spot a few other hardy souls, mere shapes in the mist, out for their morning constitutional. After circling the lake three or four times, I am rounding the curve in front of our house when I notice a lone figure approaching slowly through the mist. At first, it does not register, but as the figure draws closer, I realize it is my mother! She waves, and I hurry to meet her, shouting "Mom!" A long brown raincoat covers her flimsy nightgown.

"I just had to come meet you, Rita. Are you going around again?"

"Oh, I don't know, Mom. Do *you* feel like it?"

She is quiet for a moment, and then she winces, struggling desperately to find a strength beyond her reach. Her unflagging spirit has navigated that lake for almost sixty years—and she clearly longs to walk it one last time. But every bone and muscle in her legs can no longer carry her over that familiar path. They are shouting "No! No!" Ever so slowly, she shakes her head, looks down into the lake, and murmurs haltingly, "Oh—Rita—let's—just—walk—one another—home."

I can scarcely breathe. We turn around. Arm in arm, step by step, Mom and I begin trudging the five minutes back home. It is our last walk together here, we know in our bones, and tears well up for both of us. I can feel her chest heaving—there where our arms are so tightly interlocked. As for myself, fifty-nine years of memories crowd in on me and come streaming down my cheeks.

Our sweet home welcomes us back into the shelter of its warmth. More than ever before, it feels like holy ground to me, rich with the fullness of life lived here. Holy ground where, as a little girl, I learned not only how to walk, but how to "walk with one another." Waves of gratefulness wash over me for all my parents taught me here. And for my mother's walking …especially for her walking.

I help Mom out of the damp raincoat and into her warm blue bathrobe with the lacy cuffs. Shivering as she ties the robe at her waist, she goes straight to the stove and puts the teakettle on—as she has done every morning for sixty years.

"C'mon, Rita. Let's sit down and have a cup of tea."

"I'll Never Love You Again"

Mom struggles to live in her own retirement apartment for nearly two years after leaving her Pekin home. Gradually, however, she begins losing the ability to perform even life's simplest tasks; one by one they disappear. She no longer knows how to use the stove or how to open a can.

Only minutes away now, Dick calls to remind Mom to eat, and checks with her a couple of times a day to be sure she is taking her medication. He soon discovers, however, that phone calls are no longer enough. Her forgetfulness requires him to be there physically—every day. For months, my brother does a valiant job trying to support Mom's fierce desire to be independent. As the demands increase in frequency and intensity, however, his continued vigilance takes an enormous toll on him. Nothing is enough.

Finally, one event brings everything to a head: Mom needs a hysterectomy and is hospitalized for five days. Both of my sisters are R.N.'s. Because Patti has spent a couple of weeks with Mom pre-surgery, it's Mary's turn now. She flies in to Moline to help Mom recover and is shocked—unprepared for what unfolds. Moment by moment, Mary witnesses the irreversible damage that the trauma of surgery has done to Mom's already waning ability to take care of herself. The time we all dreaded has arrived—time to make the decision none of us kids want to make.

For three weeks following the surgery, Mary stays with Mom in the tiny apartment, changing dressings, bathing her, fixing meals, and encouraging Mom to eat. As the time draws near for Mary to return to Oregon, she and Dick make arrangements for someone to help Mom with laundry, cleaning, shopping. They hire nurses to check on Mom periodically and to help her with medications. Of course, Mom resists the very mention of outside help, scowling at a would-be helper, "Why do I need *her*?"

The day before Mary is to leave, she and Mom plan to go to Dick's morning Mass. But when Mary wakes her, Mom whispers, "I can't get up. I'm too weak." She hangs on Mary's neck, murmuring, "What will I do without you?" Indeed, that is Mary's question as well. But too weak to go to Mass? To *Dick's* Mass? Mom has gone to daily Mass for thirty years. And her son's Mass she would not miss for anything. With a chilling shiver, Mary makes Mom comfortable, drives to church by herself, and flags down Dick after Mass. "We've got to talk," she says with unmistakable urgency.

Over a quick cup of coffee, Mary anxiously confides, "Dick, Mom cannot make it this time on her own. As you know, all the laundry is done and the arrangements for help we talked about are made, but Mom turns them all away. And she is too forgetful. She doesn't even remember she had surgery. She does not eat without being reminded. The teakettle is unusable—coal-black from when she forgot to turn it off. She's burned herself badly. I'm afraid there will be a fire."

Dick knows this. "I've seen it coming" is all he can say.

Mary continues. "Mom still has diarrhea every day and she often doesn't make it to the bathroom. She cannot clean herself up anymore. And I am worried about her falling. I'm uneasy turning her over to part-time care because it will not be enough. I cannot leave her like this. She has always been an independent woman, but she simply cannot handle life on her own any longer. It's just too dangerous."

Dick nods grimly. We all had known that Mom would eventually need nursing-home care. At various times over the past months, we had toured nursing homes in the area, but none seemed to be the right fit. Now, with Mom in a crisis situation, Dick recalls that a parishioner had mentioned the Kahl Home in Iowa. He had originally dismissed the possibility because of the distance, but this current crisis causes him to reconsider.

"It is further away, across the river in Davenport," he tells Mary. "But it's the only Catholic one around, and it's run by Carmelite nuns."

"Maybe this is the missing piece," Mary says. "Mom's faith means more than anything else in her life. Maybe she could feel at home in a place where she could still worship. Please let this be the answer to all of our prayers."

Dick immediately calls the Kahl Home and learns that, despite a long waiting list, yes, today a room is open. He makes arrangements to visit that afternoon. With great reluctance, and in icy silence, Mom comes too.

Dick and Mary are pleased with the facility: it is clean, it does not feel sterile, seasonal decorations brighten the foyer and hallways, the staff is warm and friendly, there is a chapel where daily Mass is celebrated. From many of the windows, the Mississippi River can be seen rolling along.

Mom is not impressed.

Dick, Mary, and Mom follow Sister Michael, the Director of Nursing, into one of the guest parlors. "We have only the room available that I showed you. Are you interested in taking it?" Sister asks.

Dick turns to Mom in his gentle, caring way. "I think that would be a good idea, Mom. I would like you to think about moving here."

Mom refuses to look at him.

"I cannot take good enough care of you anymore," he sighs.

Mary agrees. "We can't, Mom."

"You do not *have* to take care of me. I can take care of *myself!*"

Mary persists. "Mom, you have just had surgery, and you need help right now."

"No, I do not. I don't know why you think so."

Dick's voice cracks as tears well up. "Please, Mom. I just cannot take care of you well enough."

Her son's raw feelings finally reach deeply into Mom's heart. Scarcely audible, Mom moves her lips: "Okay."

Dick breaks down and cries at Mom's "okay." It means so much to have her consent, feeble as it may be. "Thanks, Mom," he whispers.

"The next two days were hell," Mary tells me later. "Mom reneged on the 'okay' several times, shouting, 'I am not going anywhere!'" But Mary and Dick hold on to her single "okay." It is permission enough.

While packing, Mom keeps shuffling around the apartment, tearing at lids of boxes, grilling Mary, "Why are you putting my things in boxes? Why are you doing this to me?"

Mary just keeps repeating, "You need some help, Mom."

"Bullshit!"

This reply shocks Mary. Never before has she heard our mother use such language.

As Mary packs the last few things, Mom's belligerence escalates. "I had fixed her a cup of hot tea," Mary tells me later. "She began shaking the full steaming cup at me threateningly. 'Why are you doing this to me?' Her hand was trembling, and I was afraid she really might throw the hot tea at me. Never have I seen her so angry.

"Before we went to bed, I asked if she wanted to say the rosary together. I knew she wouldn't say no to that. And she didn't." (When Mom is upset, Mary knows one sure way to help her settle down: fall back on something familiar that holds meaning for her. For Mom, that would be anything concerning her Catholic faith.) "Later, Mom even let me rub her back, which is always comforting to her. But neither one of us slept well that night."

On the morning of the move, Mom is physically and emotionally unable to get up. "I can't," she keeps saying. "I'm too weak." Mary eventually manages to get Mom dressed, and she is sitting on the edge of her bed, mute, shoulders hunched, when Dick arrives.

"Hi, Mom," Dick says gently. "Are you about ready?" When he leans down to kiss her, she grabs him and hangs on to his neck as if for dear life. "C'mon, let's go, Mom," he coaxes, trying to lift her.

"Mom, please get up and walk on your own," Mary urges. "I know you can. Dick might hurt himself if he tries to carry you."

Mom lets go of Dick's neck; she would not want to hurt her son. However, she shrieks at the two of them, "Why are you doing this to me?"

And they scream back. "Because you need help! Now— you've got to get up!" After fifteen minutes of struggling— kicking and yelling and cursing and name-calling like none of them has ever been a part of before—Mom is spent. They all are. Finally, she lets Dick and Mary help her to her feet. "Mom dragged herself out of the room," Mary explained to me, "and down the long hallway, holding feebly onto the rail, groaning and gasping with each halting step, refusing Dick's outstretched arm. It was the most agonizing walk I have ever seen."

The twenty-minute ride to Kahl Home is filled with Mom's sharp accusatory questions. "Why am I going there? Why are you dumping me? I can take care of myself!" Mom, in the front seat, casts daggers at Dick and keeps turning around, glaring furiously at Mary. "Who said I needed this? Who decided? You kids?"

When Mary answers, "You need some help right now," Mom turns on her, accusing *her* of being the culprit. "You're the one who's doing this!"

Once they pull into the parking lot at Kahl Home, Mom hunches out of the car. Gritting her teeth, she draws back her fist as if to hit them. "I hate you!" she hisses. "I'll never love you again!"

"The hate, the hostility in her eyes was terrible to see," Mary recalls, her voice quivering. "Too much to bear. Too much to be the target of. I was crushed. And frightened. That moment really felt like the beginning of saying good-bye to the mother I knew."

Dick helps Mom into Kahl Home by himself. Too shaken, Mary needs time to dry her tears. Compose herself. Breathe again. Sitting in the car, she watches Dick and Mom disappear through the front doors. *Are we "dumping" her?* she wonders. *Why couldn't I take care of her? Should we have done something differently?* As she is questioning the decision, guilt begins gnawing at her.

Then, after a few moments, she heads dutifully up to Room 428.

It takes Mary and Dick an hour and a half to bring in Mom's belongings and set up her room. It will never be home, of course, and they know that, but they will make it as much like home as possible. They try to engage Mom in deciding where to put things—but to no avail. Mom remains sullen, silent, angry. They see her watching out of the corner of her eye as they place some of her treasured belongings around the room. On one wall, Dick hangs Dad's picture and two beautiful photos from Israel, one of the sun setting over the Sea of Galilee, the other of fishermen's nets like Peter must have used. On the dresser Mary arranges six tiny gold-framed graduation pictures of her kids, three on each side of Mom's beloved golden Swiss clock that chimes on the hour. A wooden carving of the Holy Family, precious memento to Mom and Dad from Dick at his ordination, rests atop the television. Her green afghan hangs over the recliner, within easy reach. On the lamp-stand next to her pillow lies Mom's blue crystal rosary.

It is about all they have time to do. Besides, the nurse has suggested they not stay long, so that Mom can settle in. When Mary and Dick turn to leave, Mom emits only a cool good-bye grunt. When they try to kiss her, Mom turns her cheek away.

Torpedoed, Dick and Mary retreat to a small earthy cafe where they order just a bowl of soup and attempt to unwind. Both are drained, unable to say much about the ordeal, except how sad they are—and how relieved. Although there is no doubt in their own minds that they have done the right

thing, that does not ease the ache in their hearts. Emotionally, both are struggling with guilt and shame. And each feels
wounded by the day's events, compounded by the week's turmoil.

Dick and Mary divide up the family calls. My brother is
informing Patti and Jerry, while Mary calls me in Seattle, where
I am anxiously waiting to hear about the move. When I answer the phone, I can tell it is Mary, but she is sobbing so hard
I can scarcely understand her. I take a deep breath.

"Mary? Are you okay? What happened? What's the matter?"

"Today was one of the hardest days of my life," she blurts
out. Recounting the traumatic details of the past two days,
she dwells especially on Mom's threat, "I'll never love you
again!"

"I am so hurt," she sobs, "even though I think she didn't
mean what she said about not loving me. I'm afraid she'll
always remember me as the one who put her in a nursing
home."

Will Mom ever speak to Mary again? To Dick? Will she
always hold this move against the two of them? I start crying
too. Feeling pretty helpless. About all I can do is listen and
assure her they *have* done the right thing. So sensitively. So
lovingly. I thank her for what she and Dick have done for
Mom—and really, for all of us.

At the same time, my heart aches for Mom. How I long to
be there with her. Or at least talk to her. I have a burning

urgency to tell her I love her. Would she rebuff me too? Probably. I don't know. I just want to be in touch. But the phone in her room is not yet connected, and I feel terribly isolated from her. Does she feel utterly alone, I wonder. Abandoned? I hope not.

I light a candle and pray for her. Just hold her and pray for her. At least there, where our spirits touch, I can feel close to her. Tears of deep deep sadness pour down my face.

Back at Mom's apartment, Mary finds herself scarcely able to pack her own suitcases for the trip home. Agitated, pacing, she is unable to throw off the piercing sting of anger and hate Mom has directed at her. She doubts she can leave on such a painful note.

An hour or two after Mary first called me, she calls again. "What shall I do, Rita? I'm flying back to Eugene tomorrow, and I just cannot leave like this. Who knows when I will see Mom again. Should I go back over? I want to, but I'm scared. I need to say a real good-bye." I encourage Mary to go over for her own peace of mind, for her own sake as well as for our mother's.

"I hope Mom will *let* me say good-bye." I hear the fear in my sister's voice, then the determination. "But you're right. If she will not say good-bye to me, I have to at least do this for myself."

After dinner with Dick, Mary drives back to Kahl Home and cautiously knocks at the open door. Mom is watching television.

Later, Mary calls me a third time, exhausted but relieved. "You won't believe it, Rita. When she saw me, Mom was pleasant. Not exactly cheerful—but not enraged, not attacking. Mellowed, at least for the moment. I did not stay long, and she did let me hug her. She even kissed me good-bye. That's enough for me."

In the weeks that follow, the painful exchanges continue, however, for my brother. He is left to deal with the aftermath alone, and Mom shows few signs of reconciling with him. Never knowing what to expect, Dick faithfully drives over to be with her nearly every day, at least for a while. Each time, Mom seems a bit more resigned, though still angry and blaming: "Why did you do this to me?" Eventually, when he stops trying to explain, Mom's words become more plaintive: "Please get me out of here, Dick. Please take me home. Please…" My brother can hardly bear it.

At some level, however, the whole family feels more at peace with Mom safely in a nursing home. But will Mom ever find that peace for herself? Will she let herself love us again?

All we can do is pray, and keep showing her how much we do love her.

The preceding three stories recount undeniable signs on the horizon—external signs of my mother's failing health that beckoned me toward pilgrimage. Inner stirrings also riveted my attention. A most compelling question began nagging the edges of my thoughts:

If I set off on pilgrimage with Mom, will I then have to face my own demons around this disease? my own shadow self filled with terror around all those fears? Am I ready for that?

I was a reluctant pilgrim here. The question gave me no peace—no peace at all, until finally I had to surrender. The following story, which takes place shortly after Mom's diagnosis, jolts me into realizing that there are changes to be made in my own life. Inner work to do. I have a long way to go...and the stakes are high.

With this encounter there is no mistaking the call. I know well the signs that propel me relentlessly forward into an inner journey. No matter how much I dig in my heels, the process has a life of its own.

But when something throws me into this much turmoil in a matter of seconds, I must no longer ignore it. Yes, it is time to face the haunting question.

The Haunting Question

A compelling urgency to do some research on Alzheimer's rises in me. As my mother begins her struggle with the disease, I must learn as much as I can. So I call the library inquiring about available resources.

"I'll pull out some of the books we have, and they'll be waiting for you at the front desk," promises the helpful voice on the phone.

I drive post-haste to the library, the librarian finds my stack of four books on Alzheimer's, and I hand her my red library card. Checking its numbers on the computer, she informs me, "It shows here that this card was reported missing. Did you lose it?"

I am bewildered. "Well..." I begin, screwing up my face, thinking out loud in an attempt to track my card's travels. "I...haven't used the card...for a couple of years...it seems..." I can retrieve no relevant information. "But... I... uh... don't...remember...losing it."

As I speak so haltingly, the librarian peers over at me strangely from her perch at the computer. "Well, we can re-issue it," she assures me, inputting the new data. When she comes back over to the counter and returns my card, there's a softening in her voice as she searches my eyes, pausing before she speaks: "Do *you* have Alzheimer's?"

I stare vacantly back.

My world starts spinning. I panic. I have no voice. I do

not know the answer. I forget who I am, where I am. Punched in the stomach. I cannot breathe. I feel nauseous. Darkness begins closing in. I hold onto the desk. Questions swirl and swirl around in my mind: *Do I? Will I? Is it genetic? How will I grow old? Who will take care of me? Oh, what will become of me?*

Eons pass. I hear sounds close by.

Suddenly I realize I have been holding my breath. So I remind myself to breathe: *Come back now. Come back. You're in the library...Yes. Yes. Okay.*

With great effort, I struggle to pull my mind and my voice back to where my body stands. But with *The Question* hanging heavily in mid-air, I avoid the librarian's eyes and I whisper, "No. No, I don't have Alzheimer's. But my mother does."

I grab the books and run back home, to the safety of my living room and the company of my sweet kitty, Abby. Gingerly, I ease myself into the cushy mauve recliner, softly kneading the armrests to make sure I am not floating away. I close my eyes, sipping only quick, short, shallow breaths.

The questions keep swirling.

The tears keep falling.

Chapter Two

GATHERING BREAD FOR THE JOURNEY

Spiritual Practices That
Sustain Me Along the Way

The following four stories take place during a long hot summer, a time I came to call "Miriam's Summer." During these months, I simply set aside the comforts of my home, my friends, and my work in the Northwest to venture into a totally unfamiliar world—the nursing home world. The troubled world of Alzheimer's. And I wondered how I would cope with being surrounded by such sadness each day.

At the time, I did not use the word *pilgrimage*. Only retrospectively did I come to realize that my time with Mom contained so many earmarks of a sacred journey, that it was indeed like a pilgrim's venture into unknown territory, with a calling to seek the profound, to live life more deeply, more consciously, with more love.

Once I accepted the signs on the horizon and knew that I needed to spend extended leisurely and quality time with my mother, I began packing. Clothes, toiletries, and lots of odds and ends. Writing materials and books. This part was easy. The true challenge was preparing myself emotionally and spiritually. What do I need to keep me going on the confusing road ahead? What shall I take with me as I set out on pilgrimage? I need sustenance more than anything, something to strengthen me.

Again, only retrospectively did I discover four major ingredients in the Bread that sustained me on my journey. I found I had to cultivate the following with care, for they fed my soul most consistently throughout this journey with my mother, and helped me walk with her and with myself more faithfully.

- Trusting the continuous work of Spirit: praying, resting in the stillness
- Seeing with fresh eyes: awareness
- Being gentle toward myself: *maitri* and breath
- Caring and deep respect: nurturing a "*Namaste* consciousness"

The following pages reflect the power of these four practices to sustain me as Bread for my journey. These stories illustrate moments when I am able to partake of this life-giving Bread.

Confession

Mom is in a funk when I arrive today, looking down at the floor with a vacant expression on her face. No light in her eyes. "I feel like jumping out the window," she says, gritting her teeth.

This statement always gets to me, and I never know what to say. I think Mom realizes that she is losing it and is depressed. She seems so lonely these days. How does she pass her time? Since she can no longer initiate certain activities, much of what used to give her pleasure is now beyond her reach. She does not read at all, has not a clue how to operate the TV or her little radio—not even how to turn them on or off. She can no longer call someone on the telephone, and is confused about how to pick it up when it rings. She dubs the view out her window just as "bare air."

"Mom, it really bothers me when you say you feel like jumping out the window."

"I just wanna go home."

I take a deep breath, trying to be patient, and we are both silent for a while.

Sometimes silence is fine, often even preferable.

"How about going for a drive in the park, Mom? You always enjoy that."

"Oh, I guess so," she says without enthusiasm.

Just as we are about to leave, Sister Leah comes to the

door. "Miriam, Father is hearing confessions today, and you are next on his list. He's almost to your room."

Turning to me, Sister asks, "Would you mind stepping out of the room for a while?"

The tail of Sister's veil has scarcely swished out the doorway when Mom hisses in disgust, "Confession! Confession! How could I have any sins to confess? All I do is sit around all day!"

Curiously, only days before, in a conversation we were having about dying, I had asked Mom if she was ready to die. "No!" she had exclaimed vehemently. "I would have to go to confession first!"

"Hmmmmmm," I mused. "Well, you probably told Sister some time ago that you wanted to go to confession."

"I don't remember that."

"You could say that today you've changed your mind. Do you want me to go down the hall and tell that to Father?" I think it is important that she knows it's okay to change her mind, to make different choices.

Silence. Then, very softly, "Well, really, I have been pretty stinky. 'Cuz I hate this place. I just wanna go home."

"I know you get upset here a lot, Mom. Feeling so cooped up. Would you want to talk to Father about that? Ask his blessing? And God's help?"

Silence again for a moment. "Yeah, I guess I could."

I am leaving for the lounge just as the priest rounds the corner to come into Mom's room. He closes the door behind him.

∽∾

I check back in five minutes only to find that the door is still closed. Also after ten. After fifteen. After twenty. Finally, the door clicks open, and I hear Father say, "Good-bye, Miriam. God bless you."

I wait awhile, and when I peek into Mom's room, I see a different woman. Eyes softly closed, she is resting calmly in her chair, green and brown afghan draped across her legs— one she knitted herself more than fifteen years ago. Her ankles are lightly crossed, hands relaxed, intertwined on her lap. She is at peace.

Mom looks up when she hears me tiptoe in. "Well, I'm ready to go now" is all she says.

∽∾

What is crystal clear in this pilgrimage is that I am not alone when I am with Mom. Not ever. I keep reminding myself of this truth. Faithfully, each day, I set aside times to pray, to meditate, to simply be quiet and rest in the stillness. Then it follows, if I am receptive and trust God's ways in such situations, I can let go of feeling pressured by a responsibility to fix things, to change Mom, or to get her to change her mind. It's not up to me! Grace intervenes and works its own miracles. How freeing that reminder is.

It is not easy, of course, to be patient through many of the struggles or conversations with Mom. I have to remind myself to pray, breathe, and to stay with her right where she is—whether it be in fun stuff or in messy emotions. If a predicament we're in somehow brings us to a peaceful place, as in "Confession," my grateful heart sings out in great wonder.

"Amazing grace, how sweet thou art."

Popcorn

A humid June evening sizzles in the heartland of America, and I am complaining to Mom, in true Northwest fashion. "It's unbearable out there, over ninety degrees! And the humidity! I can hardly stand it!"

Mom has her own agenda, however: "Well, I would really like to get outside, at least to sit in front for a while." Being cooped up all the time taxes her independent spirit to the max.

"Okay," I agree halfheartedly.

We endure scarcely ten minutes in that Midwest sauna. Mom likes being outside, but sweat is pouring down my face. I tempt her: "We can either sit out here sweltering or go back in to the cool and pop some popcorn."

"What are we waiting for?" she laughs, pushing herself onto her feet.

Popcorn wins every time. A bribe for all seasons, it was almost nightly fare for us growing up. Night owls that all of us were, late late evenings, before calling it a day, we inevitably pulled together a "midnight snack." Probably no other smell or taste brings back to us the sweetness and the saltiness of our early family life as does popcorn.

Mom and I catch the elevator up to the kitchenette, where we microwave a packet of "Healthy Choice" popcorn. As usual, she leans against the counter and peers inside, watching the miracle bag puff itself up to its bursting point. "Isn't that something!" she marvels.

Emptying the steamy contents into her all-purpose fruit-cake tin, we head to the lounge with our "midnight snack." No one else is there, so the two of us settle ourselves in soft chairs at the fourth-floor windows overlooking the lights along the Mississippi. After clinking a toast, we begin sipping our iced ginger ale and munching happily.

"I have never tasted better popcorn," Mom declares. "And it's been so long since I've had any." I say nothing. Five days ago, we had an identical party in the identical spot, but I am learning that "the facts" do not matter. Only the relationship does. To contradict her would be to break the spell, indeed perhaps ruin the evening.

Mom leans over and places a kernel in my palm. "Look at this one, Rita—how perfect it is. So puffy—it looks like a cloud." Her index finger carefully nudges the puff, turns it all around, as we scrutinize it from every possible angle.

"It does look like a cloud, Mom!"

Never before have I examined a kernel of popcorn...and I have eaten thousands, no, I'm sure, millions of them.

Mom sets me wondering: What element does popcorn have that ordinary corn does not? How *does* it pop? What spark sets those mini-explosions into motion? I've never thought about that tasty morsel as a mystery, a miracle, but I see now, it is.

After half an hour or so, I lean back, assuming we have devoured all of our treat. Mom lifts up the tin, shakes it, and checks to make sure. Her eyes get huge. "Oooooo, there are *lots* of little white pieces left!"

She proceeds to dig out the puffy tidbits, separating them on a napkin into two equal piles. We nibble our final round.

"Gosh it's fun when you come over, Rita," Mom says as she walks me down the hall to the elevator. "I am sure gonna miss you when you're gone."

A chill comes over me. "I'll sure miss you too, Mom."

God is new every morning—
God re-creates the world each day.

Streaked with rusty watermarks, a black-and-silvery plaque bearing these words hung above Mom's kitchen table for decades. Today it rests on a bamboo shelf in my own bedroom. I never thought much about that plaque; it was just always there. I wish I had asked Mom what was so important in that message that it rated such a prominent place all those years. I suppose it is a matter of looking with fresh eyes at someone, or something—like popcorn—that we've seen hundreds of times before. Passing by the same way, but without the sameness. "Waking up" at a whole new level. Giving one's attention totally to the present moment in order to meet the Mystery of whatever is transpiring.

Curiously, this kind of awareness is a spiritual practice I've been striving to cultivate for years. And sometimes I remember, but frequently I do not. Especially in this pilgrim time do I intend to be open to surprise, to look with fresh eyes, to consciously and deliberately look at a person or a situation with full awareness.

And what about the times when I forget? Well, this slightly warped and rusty plaque was nailed to the wall just below where our roof used to leak. Its bedraggled condition reminds me that nothing has to be perfect to be precious, to convey a spiritual message—including ourselves as human beings. I like that. Fresh eyes indeed.

As I set out on this pilgrimage, I certainly need a pair of fresh eyes. I have no idea where the path might lead me, and I have to trust the journey to unfold day by day, knowing it has a life of its own. I learn with my mother that I control nothing—not the onset or progression of Alzheimer's nor of any disease nor of any happening. What I also learn is that I can choose anew each day how I will meet challenges as they arise. I recall Teilhard de Chardin's words, "Trust in the slow, patient work of the Spirit." And when I remember to trust that work, that Presence, I feel a softening in my heart and in my spirit—and even in my body. I am not in charge, don't have to be. What a tremendous sense of freedom and peace and even hope this remembering brings! For then, each morning, each moment, is indeed new.

I pray to trust and to look with fresh eyes not only when I am with Mom, but when I am with anyone, anywhere. Looking at anything. At a kernel of popcorn? Yes. That new blade of grass? Yes. The tiny daisy poking up through a crack in the sidewalk? Yes, just keep looking.

So what else shall I look at in wonder? With fresh eyes? Everything, it seems…Everything.

Oops

Mom and I stop by St. Mary's this afternoon while all the nuns are away, so Mom can plunk at the piano for a while, always one of her greatest pleasures. Two weeks ago, when we dropped by, old tunes came waltzing through her fingers, especially "Easy Melody."

"This was really hot when Farley and I were dating," she had shouted over her shoulder. Then, after several attempts, she exclaimed jubilantly, "I played it all the way through!" My, how she had loved that! And what joy it gave me to see her dear figure once more bent over the keys!

Today she will have none of it. "Come on, Mom. Remember how much fun you had last time? You played 'Easy Melody' and 'Moon River' and 'Jingle Bells.'"

It's as if I haven't spoken at all. Mom refuses to step inside the music room. "I'm forgetting something," she insists. "I'm supposed to be doing something back there. I think it might have been my bath day."

(Breathe, Rita, breathe.)

"Do you want to call over and ask?"

"No...They're taking things from my room while I'm gone. I just know they are. Can we go back there now?"

"Oh, why don't you just play a little while first?" I coax, but her mood will not budge.

"Can we just go back there now?" she repeats, more stridently.

"Well, okay. Just a minute till I get some stuff...Do you have to go to the bathroom first?"

"Nope." Though reluctant to leave her alone in this unfamiliar place, if even briefly, I run upstairs to get my purse and a book.

A minute or two later I return to the living room—and there is Mom, hunched over in the middle of the room with her pants down, all wet.

"I couldn't find the bathroom."

Angrily, I snap, "I asked you right before I went upstairs if you had to go!" I'm equally angry at myself for leaving her.

Mom stands there in her half-naked state, embarrassed, hurt by my tone of voice. Wet as she is, I don't want her to sit down in one of the stuffed chairs, so I quickly pull up a plain dining-room chair and grab a towel to put over it so she won't stick to it. "Sit here a minute and I'll go get a pair of my undies for you." I wish I had not sounded so gruff...and I am reluctant to leave her again.

"Do you want to go into the bathroom first?" I still sound gruff.

"No, I don't need to." I cannot force her. Besides, the damage has already been done. While Mom puts on fresh panties, I clean up the carpet and the chair as best I can. I'm more concerned than usual, since this convent-home where I am spending the summer is not my own.

"Do you think we'd better just go back to your place now so you can get cleaned up?" After all, that *is* what she had been asking for all along, which I had simply ignored.

"I guess so."

Mom and I drive the twenty minutes in near silence. *(Breathe. Breathe.)* My mind is racing as I drive: How frustrating this is. Here I have planned a day for Mom's pleasure.

Then I begin chastising myself: Rita, don't you know Alzheimer's yet? What made you think that just because it gave her such pleasure last week, it would offer the same pleasure today? And when it became evident she was not into playing the piano, why did you push her? Here you are, following your own agenda again. Your rhythm, not hers.

In all good faith, I truly thought it was her rhythm, but what pleases Mom changes from moment to moment. I must let go of my investment in the way something I plan turns out. Learn to ride the waves of Mom's moods. And breathe.

Should I apologize, I wonder. Does Mom even remember the incident? I don't know....In her bones, she must sense something unpleasant between us, I am sure. As for myself, I know I will feel better if I do apologize. It's a matter of respect.

"I'm sorry I got mad at you back there, Mom," I finally mumble.

I don't know about Mom, but for me, the apology goes a long way. It changes the tone, clears the air between us. It's even easier to breathe after I apologize.

I get Mom safely back to her room and help change her clothes. Then I leave. Sometimes I just do not have enough energy to try and save the day.

"*Maitri*, Rita, *maitri*," I whisper to myself.

Today it is not easy to come by.

One of the practices I must remember to call upon frequently is accepting the failings and limitations of my own shadow side—often so glaring in all the "oops" times. Forgiving myself when I become irritable or lose patience with Mom. Getting off my own case. Having a humble heart. If today I am disappointed in the way I behave, well, tomorrow is a new day. Let it be a fresh start.

Nor do I have to immediately squash that initial flare of anger at myself. Rather, I can let it be, not judge it harshly. Just know there is another way, and eventually open myself to it. I apologize if I need to, and then move on. When I grant myself that humanness and that grace, I find an amazing by-product in all of this: being gentle with myself helps me be gentler with Mom and with others as well!

Buddhists name this practice *maitri*—a Sanskrit word meaning "unconditional friendliness to one's own experience." A favorite teacher of mine, Pema Chodron, describes it like this: "What makes *maitri* such a different approach is that we are not trying to solve a problem. We are not striving to make pain go away or to become a better person...Practicing loving-kindness toward ourselves seems as good a way as any to start illuminating the darkness of difficult times" (Pema Chodron, *When Things Fall Apart*, p. 25).

As I experience the softening *maitri* can bring, it becomes a precious and familiar companion. And there's another side to this coin: to acknowledge and honor the gifts I do bring, the ways I *am* caring and helpful with Mom. All the kind interactions, the playful times we enjoy. All the wondrous moments we have together. I believe this to be as important a part of creating a humble heart as looking at one's failings.

Thankfully, the practice of *maitri* is becoming almost a knee-jerk response when I am frustrated with, angry at, or disappointed in myself. And hand in hand with *maitri* goes another practice, one that, in fact, helps me *move* into a *maitri* place: breathe, deeply and slowly.

Breathe? Yes. It literally changes the air inside my lungs. Inside my being as well. It even fosters fresh eyes, an openness to Spirit work. Remembering to breathe seems so simple. And simple it is, but not necessarily easy. The challenge is remembering in the moment: *this* is a time to breathe! Don't hold your breath! Throughout the stories, I will often insert the words *(breathe, Rita, breathe)*. This is a reminder to myself when I am having a tough time, when I am anxious or at the edge of becoming impatient. *Breathe to it, breathe through it...just breathe.* Breathing this way helps a lot; in fact, it is a way of walking myself home—the most insistent of sacred callings.

Taking a moment to breathe is important in reminding me what kind of person I want to be—what kind of daughter—*right then*. It brings me "home" in that way. It quiets my mind and opens my soul—and new possibilities can then emerge. Remembering to breathe helps me ride the waves of Mom's unpredictability and agitation. Or of my own impatience and failings.

Maitri and breath. Two powerful allies in walking one another home.

Do You Know Who That Is?

A couple of times a week, as Mom and I are having supper together, we notice a middle-aged man come into the dining room. "Hi, Mom," he always says, hugging his mother, Lila.

"Oh, hi." Lila looks intently at her son, as if she knows

something, but cannot quite bring it into focus. Never does she call him by name.

Ron fusses with the napkin around his mother's neck and tells her about ordinary events of the day. "It's really hot out." Or "I'm having some car trouble."

Lila says little in response, just looks, and looks at her son some more, smiles at times, and obediently swallows each bite he brings to her mouth. When supper is over, I often see Ron and Lila stop for a while to pray in the chapel. Ron then wheels his mother back up to her room.

One evening right after Ron leaves, I hear an aide ask, out of curiosity, "Lila, do you know who that man is?"

"No," she smiles. "But he sure is nice."

• • • • •

Whew! I am grateful. It is easier to gain perspective witnessing this lack of recognition with someone else before experiencing it with my own mother. It has to be one of the deepest heartaches connected with Alzheimer's. Actually, even now, I never know for sure whether Mom knows who I am. Always when I enter her room I say, "It's your daughter Rita, Mom," just to remind her. She used to say, "Oh, I know that!" But not anymore.

How troubling this has been to Mom. How disconcerting not to know anyone around her. For how many years has she whispered anxiously to herself, "Should I know this person?" before the question finally dropped off into the vast emptiness.

At times I have wondered: *Does it make a difference whether or not I come to visit? Especially after it becomes clear that Mom no longer recognizes me, should I continue coming?* Well, watching Ron and Lila gives me my answer.

I can tell that Lila remembers something, fuzzy as that may be. Some deep memory in her bones, not in her mind—something that warms her being through and through.

In living color, I see what Ron brings: hugs and gentle touches. Simple caring. I can do that. I can rub Mom's hands with lotion. I can massage her shoulders and her back. I can fuss with her hair, dab a bit of rouge on her cheeks. Or I can just sit quietly with her. Maybe say the rosary together.

Can I take a step further into letting go? Letting go of the part of myself that's been invested in Mom knowing me, recognizing me, remembering who I am—our history and how the two of us are related. It's not easy to let that go. Could I trust that by my presence, a part of Mom deep within her spirit will continue knowing she's special, respected, and loved? A human being? A part of life?

Or perhaps Mom will *not* know that by my presence. Even so, can I at least hold that intention?

And then, what about later down the stretch? Will I be able to talk to my mother the way Ron talks to his? Will I be able to love Mom without expecting any response, any signs of love to be returned? That will be a hard one.

The first question many people ask, upon hearing Mom has Alzheimer's is, "Does your mother still know you?"

Well, sometimes she does not know who I am, but I think, like Lila with her son, Mom sees me as "nice," and knows I am someone who cares a lot about her, someone she is happy to be with. But the time is certain to come when she does not recognize even that. So then should I continue coming? Is it important to Mom? Is it important to me?

> *Without a doubt. Without a doubt.*
> *Namaste, dear Mother.*

Namaste is a greeting used in India, much as we in the Western world use "hello" or "good-bye." Roughly translated, the word means "the Spirit in me or the God in me recognizes and bows to the Spirit in you." When people in India extend this greeting to one another, they place the palms of their hands together and bow. It is a blessing, a sign of deep respect.

Respect. In its roots, *re* means "again" and *spectere* means "to look." That is what I think *Namaste* means too. To look again with fresh eyes—with caring, compassion, and deep respect. This is each pilgrim's moment-by-moment calling. Calling on the grace to see differently.

For me, then, it means to *look at Mom,* truly seeing how this precious person who is my mother is so much greater than any symptoms she exhibits at the moment. And it means to *look at myself* in a different way when I am with her. Finally, it asks me to look at this *disease* in a different way, too, not getting caught up in only its ravages, but seeing beyond to the person, the Self who is still there—to ultimately see Mom's spirit unbounded by her failing mind or shriveling body.

Namaste carries such significance for me that I have it engraved on my business cards. Next to it are words that came to me one morning in meditation: "Remember who you are. You are the Mystery, and not your history."

This message is extremely relevant in my pilgrimage through Alzheimer's, especially the "remember" part. It sparks a question I've been asked more than once: Will you continue to visit your mother when she no longer remembers who you are?

I discover a curious twist to this question. It is not *Mom* who must remember who *I* am. Rather, it is *I* who must remember who *my mother* is. Who she truly is. Not merely "an Alzheimer's patient." Nor merely "my mother." It is up to me to hold the *Namaste* consciousness: "The God in me recognizes and bows to the God in you." Keenly aware of her spirit, honoring her soul-essence. Meeting her with caring and love and respect in that sacred place of wholeness which nothing can diminish.

"The question is not what you look at but what you see," Thoreau wrote. The Spirit connection between Mom and me extends far into the Mystery, beyond the reaches of mother-daughter ties. And that is what I see.

Yes, *Namaste,* dear Mother.

PART II

⤜⤛

THE LONG ROAD

Above: Miriam Bresnahan as a young mother. She is holding daughter Rita while son Dick stands in front. They are beside the lake of *Walking One Another Home*.

Left: Miriam Bresnahan and Rita Bresnahan in the back yard of the Bresnahan home in Pekin, Illinois.

*A*s I walk this long road with my mother, what obstacles will I meet? Who are my teachers along the way? What amazing graces come to my assistance? What light awaits me at journey's end?

As I continually ask these questions during this long journey, surprise answers begin to appear when I am with my mother. A few of the following stories emerged from our long-distance telephone conversations and visits sprinkled throughout the Alzheimer years. But most of the stories arose from the extended summer I spent with Mom in 1995, when we were able to be together for several hours every day over a three-month span. At the time of these summer stories, Mom is in the middle stages of Alzheimer's, still able to think and to speak quite lucidly. She also continues to be ambulatory and fairly independent. Nearly every day she and I go outside for at least a while, if the heat is not too extreme. She especially loves going to nearby Vandeveer Park. Mainly, though, our times consist of just hanging out together at the nursing home.

I feel in my bones that Mom, as we know her, will soon be disappearing. Already her spark is fading. If even for a short summer, I hope to fill some of what she dubs "bare air" with love and laughter and singing and trees and flowers and birds and ducks—and lots of touch. I trust my presence to comfort her, in spite of the degenerative process that is chipping away at "Miriam," making her less and less available not only to herself but also to the rest of us.

Sometimes whole days go by without my catching a glimpse of the lurking Alzheimer's. Other days, that shadow eclipses Mom's every capacity.

Readers unfamiliar with this disease may be amazed at some of the details in these stories, for they convey the reality of how someone who suffers from Alzheimer's can experience opposite moods and capabilities—all within a matter of moments. Mom can go from total confusion to lucidity and back to confusion in a matter of seconds. She is frequently depressed and lonely and extremely paranoid. Non-existent is Mom's short-term memory. On the other hand, Mom's fun-loving self pops out, the joker, the observer *par excellence*. The caregiver too. Her resident philosopher catches me by surprise, and always touches me.

I continue to recognize and be grateful for how truly, how consistently, Spirit is at work as the days unfold. I am amazed to catch myself realizing, "There is nothing I would rather be doing this summer. Nowhere else I'd rather be." Daily, I pray to open myself to a deepening spiritual awareness, to keep front and center my purpose during this summer: to walk the path with Mom. It is that simple. To be with Mom, to open all of myself to the gifts of each day, each moment. To be fully where I am. I know that with this intention, I will return home a changed person—with a spacious soul more aware, more loving.

I am certainly confronted with unexpected challenges during our times together. I meet my own shortcomings face to face in startling new ways. Ways which demand a conscious effort to summon certain practices—some so key that they appear time and again in the stories. Especially staying in the present. Especially being aware. Especially focusing on the positive, on what is possible.

And so at this point, I can almost hear readers commenting, "Didn't she just say that—two stories ago?" Well, I have to learn and re-learn something until it sticks, until it becomes more consistent in the way I think as well as in the way I behave. Always there are lapses. Some things don't turn out well. But I must remind myself that I can start over again tomorrow, fresh. That comforts me a lot.

Bread for the journey sustains me throughout, especially as I learn another lesson over and over: I am not in charge here. I can only choose how I will meet each challenge as it arises. I recall Don Juan's advice to Carlos Castenada: "Look at every path closely....Then ask yourself...one question.... Does this path have a heart?"

That is what matters most. Guided by grace, again and again I renew the pledge to be faithful to the path with heart.

Part of this faithfulness, I believe, involves tapping into the healing power of telling our stories, of listening to one another's stories. In his book *Crow and Weasel* (Farrar, Strauss, 1990), Barry Lopez reminds us:

I would ask you to remember only this one thing....The stories people tell have a way of taking care of them. If stories come to you, care for them. And learn to give them away when they are needed.

Sometimes a person needs a story more than food to stay alive. That is why we put these stories in each other's memories. This is how people care for themselves.

Chapter Three

AMAZING GRACES ALONG THE WAY

As I travel this path with my mother, I become aware of how the tiniest things I do can have a powerful impact on how we relate to each other in the moment. I'm reminded of Mother Teresa's words, "We can do no great things...only small things with great love."

I find these words to ring true in countless ways. As the following stories reveal, amazing graces do lie in the small things: a telephone call, going outside with Mom, acting silly, not insisting that the "facts" of a situation be "right" from *my* perspective. I also discover how laughter and play are such good medicine for both of us.

I am always grateful when these "small things" come easily for me. And usually they seem to, especially when they are steeped in times of prayer, and when I remember to breathe. And when I trust the process, willing to stay right in the midst of what is happening between Mom and me. Oh, and also when I leave all my expectations at the door. Then, nearly always, I am surprised.

An abiding compassionate love arises from—and blesses—those times. Staying in the present moment also becomes easier when playfulness and laughter, a sense of humor and creative imagination, are invited along as companions.

How welcome these are—amazing graces indeed.

Love, Kindness, and Compassion

"I love my mother, not as a prisoner of [Alzheimer's],
*   but as a person;*
and I must love her enough to accept her as she is, now,
for as long as this dwindling may take…
All I can do is to try not to isolate her;
*   is to hold her when she is afraid;*
is to accept her as she is, as part of this family,
without whom we would be less complete."

MADELEINE L'ENGLE
SUMMER OF THE GREAT GRANDMOTHER

Afraid of Disappearing

Mother emerges from her tiny bathroom, powder puff poised in her right hand and green marbled compact in her left. In obvious distress, she stomps over to the window, where the light is brighter, and peers again into the compact. As she shakes her head, trying to clear it, fear flashes from her eyes, a fear that grows more agitated by the second. She blinks, blinks harder, straining to bring her face into clear focus.

"What's the matter, Mom?" I ask.

"I don't know. But something's wrong."

I step over to her side. Oh! She is peering into the powdery half of the compact, and the mirrored section is cupped uselessly in her palm. *No wonder she is upset!* I think to myself. *She believes her face is losing its features. She sees no eyes, nose, or lips in what she thinks is the mirror. Only rough irregular tan-colored hills and valleys that the half-used powder forms.*

"Oh, Mom, it's upside down!" I explain.

Not understanding, she moves her hand around but does not change the position of the compact.

"Here, Mom." Gently, I help her reposition the compact. "Now look. You can put your powder on."

She looks again. Mirror in its proper place, she grins at the sight of her familiar face smiling back at her.

"Ahhhhhhh," she sighs. "Thank goodness. I was afraid I was disappearing."

Flashes like these happen so fast, feed on themselves, affect her deeply. How unsettling for Mom, as well as for me, is the agitation that follows. At such times I need to remind myself: "Something is happening *inside* that is upsetting her—some fear, a skewed perception, old memories stirring up buried feelings."

Frequently I long to reach out and help Mom, remembering the countless little things she has done for me, from braiding my hair and packing my lunch when I was a little girl, to praying for me every day or helping me finance a trip home. So it is a comfort now when I can set things right, at least for the moment. I am grateful for the grace of patience this time, for the inspiration to really listen, to not disregard her words as empty chatter, to investigate, to assist her, without being critical.

I wish I could always be in that place.

What must *not* disappear in all of this is our relationship—as friends, as mother and daughter, as loving companions. For that is the essence of our journey together. I want to let go of whatever stands in the way of Mom's knowing how precious she is, how much she is loved. I pray that realizing some hidden sources of Mom's confusion—as with the compact—will bring me deeper compassion for her struggles, will help me walk with her now in her times of need. It is a reversal of roles I find sad yet sweet.

And suddenly, as I write this, tears come streaming down my face.

You know, I'm afraid she *is* disappearing.

∽◇∽

"I Can Never Find Me"

Something happens—Mom's moods shift—out of the blue. What gets triggered?

Today we are just relaxing for a while in her room, looking at the pictures in her photo album. Leisurely, we start getting ready to go over to Dick's Mass, when she suddenly becomes very negative and agitated. "I just don't care about anything anymore," is all she will say.

I wonder, *is Mom depressed?* She knows she is losing her sharpness. She knows how confused she is. But she also knows enough to be fearful, often asking, "What is happening to me?" or "What is going to happen to me?" And I have no pat answers for her—or for myself. What must it be like for Mom, living inside a mind that is slowly abandoning her? I feel sorry for her, though I try not to go to a pity place very often. Compassion, yes. That rises easily. It must be so frightening to her. It frightens me too, I must admit. Besides, I'd like to think that my presence is enough to draw her out of such feelings. It is not.

"It's been a bad day, Mom?"

"Oh, everything's wrong." She is unable to elaborate. Sometimes she is mad and doesn't know why.

Mom finishes freshening up and changing clothes. Today I brought her a new little white purse with a rose on it, and we are putting in it the things she needs for Mass–a hankie, rouge, money for the collection, her rosary, a scarf. We count them out.

Suddenly Mom begins frantically rummaging through her dresser drawers.

"Mom, what are you looking for? I think you have everything you need for Mass."

Angrily, "Yeah, everything except *me*!" She starts throwing her underwear and socks around, slamming more drawers, "I can never find *me*!"

Whew! It is time for a breather. "I'm going to walk down the hall for a while, Mom, and I'll be back..."

(*Breathe, Rita, breathe.*)

When I return in ten minutes or so, Mom is still agitated.

"We don't have to go anyplace if you don't want to," I assure her.

"But Dick is expecting us," she reminds herself, more than me.

"Then let's just sit in the chapel for a while before heading out, Mom." Church is the place where she feels most at home. She loves to pray, and often forgets to these days. Praying has a calming effect on her, and usually brings her peace if something is troubling her.

No one else is in the chapel, and we sit quietly for a few minutes. Suddenly Mom begins praying out loud: "Dear God, help me not be so mean. I'm sorry."

How consistently Spirit is at work! In surprising ways!

So I pray out loud too: "Dear God, thank you for my

mother. I love her so much. I am glad we get to be together this summer. These are hard times for her, and I'm sorry I don't understand better."

Spirit at work again!

We both just keep looking up at the altar awhile longer, quietly, until I turn and say, "Shall we go now?"

We leave the chapel and drive over to Dick's Mass.

I would like to say that those prayers changed the tenor of the day for us. Unfortunately, they did not.

Only the tenor of the moment.

"I Just Wanna Go Home!"

"Dibs on washing the dishes!" Mom reminds us as we get up from lunch at Dick's place. She still misses this simple daily chore. It gives her such pleasure.

"I love having my hands in hot soapy water, watching all those little rainbow bubbles..." Her voice drifts off momentarily... "Looking out the kitchen window..."

I can tell she has transported herself back to the Pekin house she lived in for sixty years. We talk about that beloved place as we are doing the dishes together.

It's a lazy summer afternoon. The three of us nap for a while, read the paper, watch a little Wimbledon tennis. Mid-afternoon, Dick says, "Pretty soon I need to go visit someone in the hospital."

"That means it's time for us to go too, Mom," I tell her. Dick wanders into his office, while I head downstairs to get Mom's laundry out of the dryer before we leave. "I'll be right back," I assure her.

She is alone for perhaps three minutes.

When I return, my cheery, "Here are your clothes, Mom. We can go now" is met with a cold, cold glare. Mom's mood is totally changed.

I gather up the rest of our belongings, and my brother walks us to the car. Her good-bye to Dick is stiff and forced. She waves to him halfheartedly as we drive off. But she does not look at me at all, nor does she chatter easily as usual. Miles and minutes go by. Finally, I break the silence.

"What's the matter, Mom?"

"Nothing."

"What's the matter, Mom?"

"Well, I feel like just a burden. Like I'm just in the way."

"I don't understand."

"Well, put yourself in my place. How would you feel? You're bringing me back so you and Dick can do something without me. You don't want me around."

I am shocked. I forget to breathe. Unexpectedly, I burst into tears. "That hurts, Mom. I leave Seattle to be here with you for the summer and you think I don't want you around?"

I am amazed at how easily my feelings can be hurt by her—and by such a little thing, really. But it still hurts. How can I learn not to take her comments so personally? Her paranoia rises so unexpectedly that I never get a chance to prepare myself. Will it get easier as I learn to remind myself, "This behavior is Alzheimer's in action"? How can I learn to brace myself whenever I sense its approach?

Fortunately, these episodes usually pass quickly, often within a few minutes, and are forgotten. At least by Mom.

It always takes me longer.

"Let's stop and sit by the river awhile, shall we, Mom? That always makes us both feel better."

She nods and I pull over.

Ducks scurry around, and boats motor by. We just sit quietly, absorbed in our own thoughts.

Without preface, Mom says softly, "I just wanna go home."

When she's feeling bad about something that has happened, this seems increasingly how Mom explains her behavior. For her, going back home would be the solution to any problem. And I understand her great longing to return. If only she could—I would love that too.

Now that I think about it, Mom's longing for home is not unique. I often hear residents calling out from their rooms, "Take me home. Please take me home." It breaks my heart. With the sense of urgency in their voices, their pleas seem more than a simple request. They're almost a cry, "Please help me find my way! Where am I? I'm lost. I want to go home."

"Home." What is this place in their minds they call "home," I wonder. Is it a house they actually lived in? Or heaven per-

haps? Or an elusive home they have spent their lifetime looking for? Some undefined longing for love, or for some familiar place, safe and welcoming? Their nursing-home room does
not feel like "home." So residents on Mom's floor wander aim-
lessly, endlessly, up and down the hallways in search of
"home." It is nowhere to be found.

With Mom I feel quite helpless, even guilty at times. Often I cannot comfort her.

(Breathe, Rita, breathe.)

This is certainly no time to tell her she will never return to
her house in Pekin, that, in fact, someone else owns it now.
That news would only upset her more. All I can do is be here
with her, listen to her sadness, her longing. Let her know she is
loved....Offer at least a temporary safe and welcoming haven.

I guess that is "home." I guess that is indeed walking one
another home.

"I'm Not Looking That Way"

Mom's funds are diminishing. Imminent Medicaid coverage
dictates that she must move from her familiar room in the
nursing home into a smaller room. Over the past few months,
we all—family and staff—have been preparing her for this
move. Two reasons for the move appeal to her.

"First of all, it won't cost as much, Mom. You'll save over
a hundred dollars each month!" She likes that.

"Besides that, you'll be out of the end room, Mom, where it's been kind of lonely for you. Your new room is down toward the elevator where the action is. A lot of people go by your new room." She likes that, too. Currently, she is in quite an isolated wing of the building. So we all think she is looking forward to the day the move takes place.

But moving day arrives—and Mom refuses to budge from her familiar room, refuses to set foot in the new room. "I don't know anything about moving. This one is not my room." All of her paranoia erupts, full blown.

"Nobody asked *me* about it," Mom insists. "You're always bossing me around, and I'm sick of it."

"Miriam, I talked with you about it just yesterday," says the nurse on duty.

"You did not. Just leave me alone."

Under great protest, all of her belongings are moved from Room 428 to Room 424—and Mom has no choice but to follow. For days, she is in a huff, uncooperative, and even hostile.

I am back in Seattle during all this chaos, and I wonder if a call from me will help. Her tone of voice when she answers the phone tells all. "I hate this place."

I ask about her new room.

"Nobody told me about it. And I'm not going to stay here."

"You have a view of the river now, Mom, don't you?"

"I'm not looking that way."

"Well, are you seeing lots more people go by your room these days?"

"I'm not looking that way."

No logic helps. Nor do reminders of previous conversations or of reasons she'll like the new room. I broach other topics, but she will be neither distracted nor comforted. When will I remember how useless logic and common-sense explanations and other such attempts are when Mom is upset like this? I cannot convince her.

But can't I do something to brighten her spirits?

No, I realize, I cannot.

(Breathe, Rita, breathe.)

All I can do is listen...respect her feelings, and pray.

Before we hang up, Mom snarls, "I hope this is the last move I have to make—until I go home."

"I hope it is too, Mom. I think it is."

At least the last one she will be aware of. I shudder at the next possible moves: down to the second floor, the Alzheimer unit itself, or when her dear body is carried out.

May those moves be gentler passages.

What Is It?

We are just visiting one afternoon, when out of the blue Mom says, "I'm afraid we won't have enough."

"Are you, Mom?" I respond simply.

"We've been out of it for a long time."

"Oh, have we?"

"And we really need it too."

"Well, how much do you think we need, Mom?"

"Oh, maybe five."

"Okay. I think we can get five."

"I was afraid we might not be able to get any at all."

"Oh, we can. That's a nice surprise, isn't it?"

"It sure is."

Mom's shoulders relax, her worry is gone.

What is it Mom is so concerned about? I don't know, and she cannot say. Nor does it matter. Do details need to be complete? Could I hurt Mom, fluster her all the more, if I demanded "the facts"?

Frequently, in this stage of Alzheimer's, the topic of conversation is quite irrelevant, as the ability to recall nouns is nearly nonexistent. My challenge is simple, though not always easy: remember to move into Mom's world at a time like this, trusting our relationship and our spirits to carry the day. Isn't it important for her just to know that all is well? After all, isn't it my caring that is communicated most?

I find there are such simple ways to show Mom how loved she is.

Staying in the Present: Humor, Playfulness, Imagination

"Reality is only a collective hunch."
LILY TOMLIN

Fly Show at Kahl Window

The temperature is above one hundred degrees—creating another in a string of stay-inside evenings. Mom insists, "At least I want to stick my head outside to feel the terrible heat people are talking about!" She also wants to be able to report to her friends firsthand: "It *is* just awful outside!"

We manage about ten minutes at the grotto. "Oh, it's not so bad out here, Rita," she concludes. "There's a *little* breeze—though it wouldn't knock you over."

We spend the remainder of the evening at our fourth-floor parlor window. Mom initiates some finger-shadow play in the hide-and-seek sun's rays. She creates the form of a wheel and rolls it around. Then different unnamed animals take shape, all horned or long-beaked. Her shadow animals and mine skirmish animatedly on the narrow wall between the windows.

As if on cue, a major new source of entertainment presents itself for a second evening: flies. Mom has always been fascinated by these pesky winged creatures. She tries, unsuccessfully, to corner one with the edge of a magazine.

"Those two look like they are racing each other up the window, Rita!"

We give them names: Ronnie and Rosie. We make bets on which one will win Race #1. Then comes Race #2, followed by Race #3. After ten minutes or so, the flies completely disappear.

"They're tired of racing now, I guess," says Mom.

Our attention shifts to happenings outside the window. Two huge barges are idling down the river, and there is a long, long train, complete with a classic red caboose, winding its way along the edge of town.

Then, unexpectedly, the flies return. "They just went off to change clothes," we conclude.

"It is now time for trapeze stunts!" I, as emcee, announce.

Mom's eyes continue to follow the flies intently. They loop-deloop, showing off free falls and somersaults. They perform double flips and zoom around upside down. At times, they seem to crash momentarily, brush their tails off, and resume their routine. Periodically, Mom makes appreciative sounds, "Ooooo" and "Wow," as if she were watching the *Blue Angels* themselves in action.

As quickly as before, they disappear again. "Retreating to another window?" we wonder. "To shower? Or perhaps retiring for the evening? Or maybe they just want their privacy."

Suddenly, an excited pair buzzes back over to our window. (Yes, having showered, we are certain!) One fly rides proudly atop the other, as they parade back and forth in front of us.

"What are they doing now?" Mom wonders.

"Mating!"

"Mating?"

"Well, they were courting last night—remember? They sneaked off after the show here. Ronnie probably invited Rosie down to *your* room for a sip of your chocolate shake!" We giggle at that theory.

As a grand finale, the gleeful pair hurl themselves into a steep dive, pulling up just in time to soar back toward the ceiling. The audience applauds.

Oh my. The weather is affecting our brains, I find myself thinking. *Are we getting desperate, or what—staging a repeat of last night's ridiculous "Fly Show at Kahl Window."*

Then I give it a second thought. No, it is not a repeat! Same time, same station, same company, same entertainment. But for Mom, each happening is always new, always fresh. And it can be that way for me, too, if I let it. I continue to be amazed and rejuvenated by this phenomenon. Being with Mom helps me stay in the moment, too, so that truly nothing *is* a repeat. We find ourselves becoming so absorbed in simple things, in whatever is in front of us—flies, popcorn, fountains, petunias—that time passes and we don't even notice. I am always surprised and delighted when hours pass by so quickly.

Curiously, I am seldom bored when I'm with Mom, as long as *I* stay in the now. And I remember Gertrude Stein's words, "No one real is boring." So true. The key: just be myself and walk in awareness. See common ordinary sights as if for the first time: the trees outside the window, the boats on the river, even the fly antics. Whatever presents itself. Let my imagination roam free, let my playful self join in. Be goofy. Have fun. Such good medicine!

"Bare Air"

Mom frequently points out her fourth-floor window, sighing, "Look, all you see is bare air out there. No trees, no birds, nothing. Just bare air." No wonder Mom's most frequent response to my question "What would you like to do today?" is "Oh, I'd just like to get out."

This late Saturday afternoon, Mom is in fine fettle when I arrive, willing to risk being sprinkled on (as the weather forecast predicts) for the opportunity to "get out." I've brought chicken sandwiches along, so we drive to the park for a picnic, heading toward where her pet ducks usually hang out. Sure enough, there they are—only twenty yards from our bench: Mother Duck with seven of the busiest balls of fluff, splashing about in a huge puddle. "Don't they go lickety-split?" Mom laughs as they race on the cement along the edge of the lake.

Mom's alertness perks up notches when she's outside. I see how important it is to help her experience different environments, to stimulate her senses. She loves to be where the action is; she loves to people-watch. Today she laughs at the kids playing by the water and coos at a baby being wheeled by in a stroller. She turns toward and comments on every sound, from quacks and arf-arfs to the traffic in the street to planes in the sky.

Nature is wondrous in Mom's eyes. The trees and the grass and the flowers hold a particular awe for her. Her most favorite refrain is a variation on the tree theme: "The trees, oh the trees...Aren't they pretty? Look at that one. It is almost touching the ground." Here again is that gift of appreciating what is right in front of us. Simple everyday things.

When the ducks paddle off to the other side of the lake, I ask, "Shall we go over and sit by the fountain awhile, Mom?"

"Let's do!" We wend our way over to the ancient fountain and sit down close by on a dilapidated bench. A warm breeze is billowing rainbow sprays away from us, and a few stray droplets sprinkle us. We don't mind at all. We sit by the fountain silently at first, arms wrapped around each other at the back of the bench, watching brilliant sunset rays cycle through splendid sprays and gushes. During one of the tall slender gushes, I start humming a song I often think of when I'm with Mom: "Sweet and Low." It's an old favorite, and she sings along with me.

On the way "home" in the car, and walking along the halls toward her room, Mom is humming again! How heartwarming to see light dancing in her eyes again, to hear the lilt in her voice. Her senses have been sparked, fed, renewed; her heart as well.

From Mom's "bare air" fourth-floor perspective, I begin to understand more clearly the urgency of her request, "I'd just like to get out for a while."

What a Difference a Call Makes

Mom's voice is scarcely audible when I call this particular Sunday from Seattle, where I've returned for a few days to settle some business.

"I don't feel good," she tells me.

"What's the matter, Mom? Are you sick to your stomach? Did you go down to lunch? Would a nap help?" I ply her with questions. Not a good idea, especially the factual ones. They fluster her all the more, even irritate her. Nevertheless, I steamroll on: "Did you tell the nurses?"

"What nurses? There aren't any nurses here."

"There are some close by, Mom. If you're not dizzy, you could walk down to the nurses' station and tell someone there you don't feel well."

"The nurses' station?"

"You know, where all the windows are, where they give you your pills."

"I don't take any pills."

"If you go to your doorway, turn right, and walk a few steps..." Way too many directions. Besides, by now I should have gotten the hint about her present state of mind. I did not.

"The nurses' station is right by the elevator, Mom."

"The elevator?"

(Breathe, Rita, breathe.)

It finally dawns on me: try another tack. I don't want to force it, but perhaps I can initiate a mood swing.

"Is it hot and sunny there, Mom?" I figure in Illinois it's always hot and sunny in July.

"No, it's icky out. And I'm really cold."

"Do you have your white sweater on?"

"I do. But I'm still cold."

"Well, I have an idea. It is very sunny and hot here, way too much for me. So I am just gonna send some of that heat and sun *your* way. Okay? I'll blow our hot air across the telephone lines and you will feel warm and toasty all over. Wanna do that?"

"Yeah. I'm really cold."

"Let's see what we can do about that. Are you ready?"

"Yep."

"Well, just sit back in your chair now and close your eyes." I pause. "Take a couple of deep breaths, Mom, and relax."

We have done this kind of visualizing before, drawing upon our imaginations to help Mom feel better. When she has had a sore shoulder or some other ache, I have "massaged" her from a distance. She really gets into it. It makes her feel better, she says, and we usually end up laughing.

I begin blowing slowly, audibly, into the receiver, sending her my love as well, along with the warmth of each breath. In between some of the breaths, I say something like, "Imagine the sun streaming in through your window. It is warming your feet...your hands...your back...the top of your head....It feels so good."

After a couple of minutes, I pause, and Mom jumps right in. "Oh my, wait a minute," she laughs. "I have to go get my hankie. Sweat is pouring down my face!"

Easter in the Air

A long-standing tradition has been for Mom and me to spend the days around Holy Week and Easter together. It is one of Mom's favorite times. Whenever I come to visit during this season, I bring silly things—the two bunny noses, for example, that we nearly suffocate under. Nevertheless, we put them on when we go down in the elevator or when we appear at Dick's door. (He never recognizes us.)

Then there is the eight-inch, pink plastic bunny that lays jelly beans when we push down on her head and say, "Please lay an egg, Rosie!" The staff loves this one, too. Each time one of them comes into Mom's room, Rosie produces a couple of jelly bean eggs.

To top off the fun, I have brought matching plastic bunny rings for us to wear. Mom and I flash these on our fingers the whole week, showing them off at meals, at church, or at the park. They are the envy of her buddies.

We make Easter baskets and hang "Happy Easter" greetings at her door and on her window. As we are decorating her room, I ask, "What's your favorite thing we do when we are together, Mom?"

"All the laughing."

"You mean with the bunny stuff?"

"Yeah. And all the other laughing."

Mom loves the Holy Week liturgy, and since the nursing home is only fifteen minutes from her priest-son's parish, we drive over to services there.

"I still cannot believe that is my son up there," she whispers proudly (and a bit too loudly) when Dick comes out to the altar in his vestments. She follows his every move, craning her neck to keep him in sight. She prays all the prayers by heart, and sings lustily the hymns that are familiar.

On Holy Thursday, during the "washing of the hands" ceremony, it is a touching moment for both of us when Mom washes my hands and dries them reverently, and I do the same with hers. Afterwards, we stay for the Bread Feast. She samples the delicious breads, sips her coffee, and greets the parishioners, many who gather around, telling her, "We love your son. What a wonderful mother you must have been."

Mom just glows and smiles modestly. "Well, I didn't do it alone."

On Easter morning, Mom and I drive over to Dick's special Mass. She is sporting a new Easter outfit: soft blue slacks, and over her delicate pink shell, a satiny white blouse with vividly colored daisies. A white sweater vest. She rubs her hands appreciatively up and down the soft material gracing her legs, and slides her hands along her arms. "I feel so good—so dolled up."

Mom then pauses a moment, ponders, and asks, "Is today Thanksgiving?"

A Leaf Falls

It is an unusually warm September day, and I am back in Illinois for Mom's birthday celebration. As she and I are sitting out in the sun, over and over she exclaims, "Oh the sun feels so good on my back...It feels sooooo good."

We stay outside all afternoon, she loves it so. A couple of times I push the wheelchair around so she can visit her favorite places—the Blessed Mother shrine, the parking lot trees, the late-blooming petunia beds. Mostly though, we sit quietly and simply watch leaves fall...watch leaves fall...watch leaves fall.

Sometimes we squint up at treetops, trying to catch a single leaf as it breaks free. I have never before been privileged to witness that millisecond release.

The leaf simply lets go... so easily...

"Here comes one, Mom. See that one?" Our eyes follow the slow, meandering, floating, sometimes spiraling descent.

"Where is that one going to land, Mom?"

"Oh, right there," she guesses, pointing toward a sunny spot.

We watch intently. Does it drop out in the sun? Or into our shadows?

"Oh, it fell there in the crack!"

When a slight breeze stirs, three leaves come scratching up the driveway and swirl around our feet. We marvel at their dance, their leafy music. Laughing, we lean over and stretch out our legs, trying to catch a leaf with our toes.

I find myself wondering, *How long has it been since I just watched a leaf fall? Ever?* I want to rest more often in this kind of awareness—not only when I'm with Mom. I want to treasure the great wonder of bringing myself fully into this moment...this precious moment.

Is there a greater gift I can give myself? Or Mom? Or whomever might be my companion at the moment?

Chapter Four

AN UNEXPECTED GUIDE ALONG THE WAY

Pilgrims frequently speak with great fondness and even awe of teachers they meet along the way, those who open up their minds and their hearts, helping them face what lies ahead. In this pilgrimage with Mom, I often find myself wondering, *Could it be that in her Alzheimer's, Mom is teaching me something profound, even something of the essence of life?*

Not always have I been open to the possibility that Mom had wisdom to share with me—certainly not as an adolescent, nor even as a young adult. That both Mom and I are such strong-willed, stubborn women often got in the way of our relationship. Over the last twenty-five years or so, however, that has markedly changed. Especially now, it has become crystal clear that my mother is indeed my teacher. And my decision to receive her teaching with an open heart makes all the difference to me in this journey: I am able to *listen* to Mom from a deeper place. I then listen to *myself* there too—and to God's voice as well. It feels like throwing open a window to let in the fresh air of awareness. I am grateful.

When I was a young girl and someone gave me a gift, Mom always prompted, "What do you say?" From her, I first learned to say "Thank you." Even more, she taught me how to live in a grateful spirit, to appreciate the little things as well as the big. The story "I Count My Blessings" brings me to these questions: What can help me remember to carry that piece of wisdom with me: to count whatever blessings are still mine? Here Mom is in a nursing home, enduring countless losses, yet her attitude is nearly always a positive one. In fact, "thank you" are the words I hear her speak most frequently.

And she is constantly surprised—by flowers that have been in her room for days, or by visitors who just step out of the room for a while. "Oh," she exclaims, smiling broadly at their return, delighted to see them as if they have just come. She lives David Steindl-Rast's words: "An inch of surprise can lead to miles of gratefulness."

I intend to welcome into my own life more of this surprise-gratefulness combo. Also I will continue to challenge myself: How can I shift the spotlight of my awareness away from regret, away from what I can no longer do, from what I no longer have? And then very deliberately focus that spotlight on the many gifts of life I do continue to enjoy?

Mom's abiding gratefulness and playfulness, and her gift of staying in the present speak powerfully of what truly matters. Again and again, Mom teaches me directly by her own actions these special qualities of a pilgrim spirit. I pray for the grace in my own life to match her faithfulness.

This old woman…
isn't my mother,
is not what I think.

She's a spiritual master
trying to teach me
how to carry my soul lightly
how to make each step
an important journey,
every motion and breath
anywhere
as though anywhere
were the center
of the earth.

BETSY SHOLL,
MOTHERS AND DAUGHTERS, P. 245,
EDITED BY TILLIE OLSON

Gratefulness

Gratitude is the heart's memory.
FRENCH PROVERB

An Attitude of Gratitude

Mom and I are seated at a guest table in the nursing-home dining room, polishing off our noon meal of barbecued ribs, sauerkraut, and mashed potatoes. We've both eaten with relish, especially Mom, who has always loved gnawing on bones.

When Wendy comes to clear the table before presenting dessert, Mom looks up and says, "Thank you! That was a delicious meal!"

Wendy nods and turns away with the tray of dirty dishes. Giggling, Mom elbows me, confiding in a whisper, "You know, it was delicious—but I don't even remember what I had to eat!"

Better Than a Pot of Gold

"How about driving over to the Mississippi tonight where the guys are fishing?" I suggest to Mom.

"Oh, that would be great!"

As we step out the door for our little jaunt, we wave to

Sister Michael, telling her we are heading off "in search of fame and fortune." She laughs.

At the river, we find a bench in the shade only a few yards from the action, and settle in. The casino paddle boat on the opposite shore is just departing, its calliope strains filling the air. We hum along with "By the Light of the Silvery Moon" and other favorites until the boat paddles out of earshot.

Then the fish start biting. Channel cat—two small ones come flying out on one line, followed by a four-pounder (which the fisherman deems "small"). Both Mom and I exclaim, "Wow!" before whispering to each other, "Poor little thing."

We begin reminiscing about how my brother Jerry, when he was a little boy, used to fish at the lake across from the house, sitting patiently for half the day or more. Mom would peek out the window periodically just to see that he was okay. Sometimes I would take him a little sandwich and some lemonade, if he hadn't fixed something for himself. And I'd just sit with him awhile on the warm cement step and watch the cork bobbing up and down in the murky water.

Early in the morning, Jerry would cook up his dough ball to just the right consistency, add a little cinnamon, wrap it in wax paper, and confidently set off across the street, bamboo rod over his shoulder. After hours had passed, he would march proudly home with his catch. "Cleaning them would smell up the whole house," Mom recalls. He would fry them up himself and have a feast, with bites doled out to those of us who pleaded...or were brave enough.

I've noticed that even though Mom may forget what happened a moment ago, she can whisk herself effortlessly, with just a little nudging, back across decades. Reminiscing is one of our favorite pastimes.

One of the young fishermen—in his mid-twenties maybe—drops back to Mom and me, holding out a little packet for us to sniff. It smells sweet, "like Kool-Aid" is his description. "I just got this. It's bait. You dip the worm in it—the fish love it."

"Do you ever make dough balls?" Mom asks.

"No I don't. I heard you talking about it though." Pause. "I wonder if *my* mom ever talks about *me*, if she remembers how I used to fish when I was a boy…Probably not." He pauses, before murmuring, "I never see her," and steps back to tend his poles leaning against the river wall.

As Mom and I get up from the bench, the young fisherman calls over, "You coming back here tomorrow?" I shrug my shoulders. "Aw, come on back tomorrow night!" he urges. Mom and I both grin.

A "turtle" apiece is waiting for us back in Mom's room. We savor this delectable caramel-pecan-in-chocolate concoction—her favorite candy—as we perch at the fourth-floor window watching, this time from a distance, the same casino boat returning and docking.

Well, we did not find fame on our venture tonight, but we did find fortune. Paddle boat. Calliope music. Fishing action. Young man talking about his mom. Sweet reminiscences.

Mother and daughter, hand in hand, bathed in a brilliant summery sunset. A nearly full moon rising in the opposite sky.

Better than a pot of gold.

I Count My Blessings

It is always a mixed experience, eating supper with Mom in her dining room. Residents with guests are isolated at a separate table, distanced from the others, behind a huge concrete pillar. This arrangement always peeves Mom.

"I can't *see* what's going on!"

Besides, Mom is such a social creature. "I want *both* of us to sit at the table where I usually am!" This frustrates her. She wants to eat with me, yet she's afraid of missing out on something with her friends—and she is afraid of hurting their feelings by not sitting with them.

This particular evening, Mom and I are seated close to the door. In no hurry to leave, we observe the parade of residents leaving the dining room. "Look at that poor woman," Mom observes, a bit too loudly. "Her legs always have to be straight out...Oh, and that one—she can't even lift her head up."

Ninety-eight percent of those who pass by are in wheelchairs, a few, with great effort, wheeling themselves. Some wave to Mom as they go by. Perhaps half a dozen use walkers, and four or five get around under their own steam.

"I sure am one of the lucky ones at my age," Mom says as the rest of the residents file by. "My legs still work, kind of."

"You are lucky."

"Everyone is always saying they wish they were me. They wonder how I stayed so healthy."

"Well, how did you, Mom?"

"Oh, I don't know. I always walked a lot, and still do here. All around the hallways every chance I get."

"Walking has always been important to you, hasn't it?"

"Mhmm."

Mom reflects for a moment and adds, "Besides, I'm Catholic. So I have that. And my kids."

"You *are* lucky, Mom."

"Yep," she adds, as she pushes herself away from the table. "I count my blessings every day."

Focus on What Is Possible, Rather Than on What No Longer Is

When the heart weeps for what it has lost,
the soul rejoices for what it has found.
SUFI VERSE

A Ministry

After waiting and waiting for Mom to return to her room, I finally set out to find her. And there she is, in her neighbor's room, having forgotten all about my coming over.

"This lady's been real sick, Rita," she explains, "and I was just helping her."

Mom has always been a "helper," has always loved being of service in whatever way she could. She would drive her cronies to Mass, wrap bandages at the Red Cross, work in the blood bank, distribute food for Share. In fact, her identity has been tied quite strongly to serving others.

Not being able to help people has been one of Mom's greatest challenges in the nursing home. In those first difficult months, she said things I have never in my sixty years heard her say: "I just hate myself." "I am so ashamed of myself." "I feel so useless, I just sit here and I don't do anything good for anybody."

Over time, however, this mood has gradually changed.

Mom has gotten into a rhythm, I notice. After meals, she pushes a resident or two back to their rooms. "It's so much easier when I push too," she explains.

Mom gets many requests from those who cannot walk, which is almost everyone. She is frail herself, and, although saying no is not easy, she is surprisingly able to draw the line: "No, I'm sorry (always 'I'm sorry')," she will say, "but I can't do that." I am amazed, and relieved, that she understands her limitations.

"You know, I think you have a ministry here at the Home, Mom," I say to her this evening.

"What do you mean?"

I point to the plaque on the opposite wall, and I read aloud its words:

Certificate of Appreciation
to
Miriam Bresnahan
with gratitude for your gift of time and self
as
Coordinator of St. Joseph
Nursing Home Ministry
1984-1991
– Sister Charlotte

"Remember all those years you went to two nursing homes twice a week! You were eucharistic minister there for sixteen years! You would bring communion around, and gather the people together to say the rosary."

"Oh, those poor people were always so tickled to see me, Mom recalls, "and it made me feel good too." She pauses. "And now here *I* am."

"Mhmm, who would have believed it?…Well, here is what I mean about having a ministry in this place. Your neighbor Hazel told me the other night: 'Miriam is the main one I can count on as a friend here. I'm new, and she's so nice to me.' In fact, lots of people here tell me how much they appreciate you."

"They do?"

"Yes, they do! You give others a hand if they need it. I see how friendly you are, how you touch people on the shoulder or the arm, how you make them feel good, how they are often laughing when you're around…." I am realizing how important it is for Mom—and for myself as well—to focus on these gifts of hers that remain intact.

She is incredulous. "I do all that?"

"You do! It *is* a real ministry here."

She likes that idea.

"Is She Crying?"

Mom, Patti, and I are scrunched in Mom's tiny living space, singing along with some oldies Patti's brought to play on her boombox—songs like "Roll Out the Barrel," "You Are My Sunshine," "Let Me Call You Sweetheart," "Row, Row, Row Your Boat."

Suddenly, the door swings open and an aide pushes Mom's roommate over to her side of the room, braking the wheelchair next to her bed. We wave to Margaret and sing on.

But Mom's eyes keep drifting over to her roommate. Suddenly Mom stops singing right in the middle of "How Great Thou Art."

"Is she crying?" Mom asks.

"It looks like she is."

"I wonder why she's crying."

"I don't know. It's just after lunch. Maybe she's tired and wants to take a nap."

"Oh." We try to draw Mom's attention back to singing the oldies, but in another minute or two she interrupts and asks again, "Is she still crying?"

"Mhmmmm."

"I wonder what's the matter."

I finally get it. Mom's ministering and caring self is on high alert.

"Well, would you like to go over and find out?"

"I sure would."

I push Mom's wheelchair over next to Margaret's so they are alongside and facing each other. I help Mom reach her hand out so she can touch Margaret's arm. That's always been such a natural gesture for her.

"Her name is Margaret, Mom," I whisper. "You can just say, 'What's the matter, Margaret?'"

"What's the matter, Margaret?"

Margaret sobs, "Oh I'm trying as hard as I can. I'm trying as hard as I can."

"I know you are, Honey, I know you are." No coaching needed here.

"I'm doing the best I can."

Mom pats Margaret's arm. "I know you are, Honey, I know you are."

I tiptoe back over to Mom's side of the room, no longer a part of their world. The two of them nod back and forth a couple of times, exchanging a few more words. Although unintelligible to me, at some level they seem to be communicating and understanding each other.

After a minute or two, Mom looks over her shoulder to where Patti and I are standing—and gives us a "come help me" look. Margaret is still crying, though more softly.

"Tell her that she'll be able to take a nap pretty soon," I whisper to Mom.

"You'll be able to take a nap pretty soon."

"And tell her good-bye for now."

With a final pat-pat, Mom says, "G'bye for now."

Sure enough, the aides return only minutes later and put Margaret to bed, her crying and moans gradually fading. Mom turns in for a short nap as well, and soon I hear deep contented sighs coming from both sides of the room.

As for me, I feel privileged to have witnessed this Two-Minute Life Lesson: "How to Simply Be With Another Person." All the ingredients of this most spiritual of practices are there: full presence, compassion, connection. No need to take Margaret's pain away. No judgment. No need for lots of words. Just listen. Just be with her. Gentle touch. All Bread for the journey—the essence of walking one another home.

So Margaret was walking Mom home as well? Oh yes. It's seldom just one way. For Mom is once again able to express her ministering self. That has always been such a "home" for her: feeling that she has something to give, that she can make a difference. Later today she may not even remember this exchange, and Margaret won't either. But, somehow, I am convinced, in their brief moment of connection, both Margaret and Mom felt their beings warmed deep down where they live.

School Days, School Days

Holding hands, Mom and I stroll along the sidewalk in Vandeveer Park toward the big maroon steel bench we always claim. Mom begins swinging our hands and singing, "School days, school days, good old-fashioned rule days. Reading and writing and 'rithmetic..." With great animation, she sings the song all the way through, missing only an occasional word.

"Gee, I wish I could still skip," she says. So she tries. "Aw shucks, I can't anymore." Then I try. But neither of us can get either leg a-hoppin'. We giggle at ourselves.

Well, maybe our legs don't work so well, but our arms still swing and our voices still carry a fine tune. Each day of this journey I am learning to be grateful for little things Mom and I enjoy—stuff I previously might have taken for granted. We *can* delight in soft summer evening breezes, sitting together on this bench by the fountain. We *can* marvel at the changing shapes of the water making rainbows in the air—slender, misty ones, followed by tall, powerful gushes reaching up toward the sky. As we idle the afternoon away, both Mom and I find these simple pleasures refreshing, working a kind of magic on us.

Seeing with fresh eyes. Gifts do abound!

Tangles

"Hey, Mom, can you untangle this necklace for me?"

How many times, when we were growing up, did Mom hear this plea from her daughters. We would be fuming, pulling at the offending jewelry, ready to dump it, when it would dawn on us, "Oh, I bet Mom can get this knot out." Without fail, she was able to do just that—even welcoming the challenge.

First, Mom would sit down and peer deeply into the knotted strands, squinting to follow their errant meanderings, try-ing to discern—"Is it one knot or several?" Then meticulously and with enormous patience, she would jiggle and gently pull and jiggle the tangle some more, sometimes putting soap on it or fetching a needle, maybe tweezers, to aid her in the task.

At times, it would take Mom up to fifteen minutes or even half an hour, but she was both confident and tenacious, re-fusing to give up until, with a triumphant, "There!"—she could wave the now free-flowing jewelry high in the air. It was then her privilege and her pleasure to fasten the necklace around the neck of its grateful owner.

Now here we are, Mom at age ninety and me at sixty-two, sitting together at the edge of her tiny bed in the nursing home, gray heads bent over my slightly tangled sterling-silver chain. Mom's eyes lit up tonight when I placed my necklace in her hand saying, "Could you please try to get this knot out for me? You've always been so good at that!"

"Sure!" Mom responded without hesitation, sitting taller, pleased to be asked to do me a favor. Untangling is one of the few talents Mom can still call upon and trust to be there. To-night she goes at the knot in my chain with a vengeance—the same old vengeance—although some of the former confidence is missing. She sets her jaw and squints her eyes, determined to find the path, the precise point of entry. I just breathe with her.

Looking on, I recall that medical research labels the ab-normalities in the Alzheimer brain as "tangles." Daily I watch

Mom's futile attempts to disentangle the pathways in her mind that are knotting ever more tightly by the moment. She is more successful with my silver chain, however, in spite of fumbling gnarled fingers. "There!" she declares proudly, waving it over to me.

"Hey! You have done it again, Mom!"

There's Still Something Left!

"I've lost all my words," Mom complains to me one day, in great dismay. Frequently, she can't think of the word for some simple ordinary object like *towel* or *window*.

"You still use quite a wonderful vocabulary though, Mom."

"I do?" She does not believe me. "All right then, tell me next time you hear me use a big word."

The next day I am reporting the weather to her in the morning before I come over: "It's ninety-four degrees out!"

"We ought to hibernate!" Mom exclaims.

I shout through the phone, "Hibernate! That's one of those big words, Mom! And in the past week you have used 'stagnate,' 'indicate,' 'remarkable,' and 'outstanding'"!

"But did I use them in the right way?"

"Yep. And the other day you told me you had a 'premonition' about the weather. You also commented that I needed the right 'environment' to write in!"

"I did?"

Mom seems surprised and pleased. "So there's still something left then?"

"There sure is!"

I cannot deny that my mother wrestles with paranoia, and that her short-term memory is all but nonexistent. Several times each day she asks, "What day is today?" I watch as she hangs up the telephone, placing the receiver sideways (like her old one). Soon the busy signal begins its annoying buzz, and she does not know how to make it stop. She cannot remember appointments, times I am coming, or when anything else is happening, even if she has just been told or I write it down for her and place the message in a conspicuous spot. She retains no facts, even the most familiar.

Curiously, though, much of Mom's advanced vocabulary remains intact. She can still carry on a conversation, and she still recognizes me—usually. I enjoy the moments when those capacities appear. Acknowledging these, reminding Mom as well as myself, is uplifting for both of us.

I do find that I have to catch myself, however. Because her short-term memory has vanished, and she is frequently unable to retrieve the simplest of words, I assume at times that most of Mom's other intellectual capacities are lost as well. Actually, she is much more "with it" than initially meets the eye. And then—sometimes much less. As I spend extended time each day with her, I am discovering this truth.

There's still something left then?

Absolutely!

Chapter Five

OBSTACLES
ALONG THE WAY

Fortified by the Bread for my journey, I set out on this pilgrimage, confident that I knew what would be asked of me, and how I hoped to respond. I did not dream that the changes Mom would experience as a result of Alzheimer's would be so dramatic and unpredictable from day to day. Nor had I anticipated meeting my shadow side, my own stumbling blocks, so quickly or so frequently.

Some people seem to be infinitely patient. Others—easy-going, and flexible. They can let go of expectations, of their own way of doing things. For some, remembering to take care of their own needs is not a problem. Nor is pacing themselves.

You know, I envy them. For it is these very challenges—to

my patience and feelings of guilt, to self-care and pacing my-self, and to being flexible and letting go—that call for the greatest effort on my part. These challenges catch me off guard, time after time, as I beg a gracious Spirit to come to my assis-tance, to help me let go—of control, of structure, of having to be right—which then can allow space for me to just be with what is happening.

Let's face it. The loss of one's mental capacity is stressful for everyone involved. At times, simple daily activities such as eating, talking, and going to the bathroom become com-plicated and even agonizing. In dealing with these details, help is needed in more ways than one. Stephen Levine's words from *Meetings at the Edge* frequently resound in me: "The only work you have to do is on yourself."

Am I willing?

THE FIRST CHALLENGE:
To Patience and Feelings of Guilt

Grant me the serenity to accept the things
I cannot change,
the courage to change the things I can,
and the wisdom to know the difference.
REINHOLD NIEBUHR

Fresh Air Works Wonders

"Let's make tonight a popcorn night!" we agree over the phone. I often call Mom in the morning just to check in, especially if I'm planning to go over to see her later than usual.

When I walk into her room that evening, however, the stale smell of urine is overpowering. Mom is trying furtively, futilely, to wash her slacks in the tiny bathroom sink. Surely she must realize this does not take care of the problem.

"You didn't make it to the bathroom in time, Mom?"

Defensively, "I made it every time." Pause. "Why, do I smell?"

"Well, your slacks do. How about putting on something fresh and going over to the park? I can just throw those slacks in the washer when I get home."

"What slacks?" she hisses through pursed lips.

"Your brown ones, Mom. Let me take them."

"They're fine. They're dry."

Mom rejects any offers of help, and I do not want to strong-arm her—it is not worth the fight. So, for tonight, those slightly-rinsed-but-still-smelly brown slacks remain hidden back there somewhere in her closet, covered over by blouses and who knows what else. I hope "Laundry" finds them.

"The slacks you have on need changing too, Mom."

"No! They're clean!"

"They are not, Mom. Please take them off and put on a clean pair."

I pull out a pair from the closet. "Here. Here is a clean pair."

"Everyone's always telling me what to do! Do you think I can't take care of myself? Just leave me alone!"

(Breathe, Rita, breathe.)

I offer to help Mom wash herself, saying, "That's such an awful feeling."

Her "I am fine!" convinces me to keep my distance.

Angrily, she slides the offending slacks off, and begins putting the blue ones on, but over soiled underwear. Reluctantly I remind her, "Mom, be sure to change your undies too." I move toward the drawer to find a clean pair, but she pushes me aside, muttering fiercely under her breath.

I go into the bathroom, purportedly to use it, and manage to clean it up a bit. When I emerge, Mom has changed her slacks, but glares at me, shouting, "There! Are you satisfied?"

I do not know what to say. I feel so helpless.

(Breathe, Rita, breathe.)

Dealing with this has taken half an hour or so, and we are both tense and agitated and exhausted. What now? Saying nothing is sometimes the best I can offer.

We are quiet for a while, then tentatively I ask, "Do you want to do anything special tonight?"

Mom just sits mutely, angry and ashamed, in her chair. Even popcorn is out of the question—for either of us.

"What about going outside to sit by the Blessed Virgin statue for a while, Mom?"

No response.

I wait a minute, quietly, then coax a bit more. "Let's go outside."

Grudgingly, she agrees.

As we walk along the halls, Mom drags her feet more heavily than usual. I do too. I wonder, *Is this worth fighting over like we are?* I don't know. Sometimes I feel guilty about it all.

The two of us step outside into the cool night air and ease ourselves onto white lawn chairs facing her favorite statue of Mary, spotlighted in the small grotto. Slowly, her blue rosary begins its familiar journey through tired and swollen fingers. For Mom, there is something profound in repeating familiar religious prayers. They seldom fail to bring her a sense of calm, of peace, of feeling "at home," at least inside herself. I, too, am learning to count on that grace. It is always there, I must remind myself.

As Mom's shoulders begin to relax, she heaves a few deep sighs. I take a couple of deep breaths with her, and echo one of her favorite sayings: "Fresh air works wonders, doesn't it?"

You Never Know

The incontinency scene from last night left us both upset, so today I arrive at Mom's somewhat hesitantly. She is still at dinner, but after a few minutes, she breezes in, scarcely greeting me before she says, in a little-girl singsong way, "I had an ak-ki-dent."

Rather nonchalantly, she takes off her britches and puts on clean ones, undies and all. I stand there in amazement. How puzzling are the sweeping changes in her mood from one day to another, from one moment to another. I never know what to expect.

I see my chance. "Why don't I just take these home and put them in the washer there, Mom. It will be so easy." I brace myself for the barrage of anger like yesterday's.

"Okay," she agrees cheerily.

Pushing my luck, I add, "Maybe your brown slacks too."

"Okay."

I dig them out from the pile of blouses Mom hid them under toward the back of her closet. "Laundry" could never have unearthed them. I find other grungy treasures too that she lets me take without protest.

I put them all in a bag, out of sight, before Mom changes her mind.

You never know. You just never know.

Questions, Questions

"I feel kinda woozy," Mom tells me after lunch.

"Why don't you take a little nap, Mom. I'll nap too—here in the chair."

"Okay." She doesn't want to get under the covers, so I throw her little green afghan over her.

Seldom have I known Mom to lie down in the middle of the afternoon. Sit in a chair and fall asleep, yes, but to actually lie down on her bed is radical. Today she falls into a long deep sleep. I doze with one eye open. When Mom awakens, she looks around and sees me there close by, reading. At first she doesn't know who I am or where she is. I tell her.

"Oh, I know that!"

She is full of other questions:

"Is it morning?"

"What time is it?"

"Have I been up today?"

"What day is it?

"Did I pass out?"

Out of habit, she looks at the digital clock on her dresser and reads aloud the large red numbers: "3-2-7." Pause. "What does that mean?"

Although I answer her questions very simply, she repeats most of them again...and again...and again. Impatient with herself by this time, she starts to sit up.

"Why am I sleeping in the middle of the day?"

"You have been really sick these last two weeks," I remind her, "and you need this extra rest."

"I was sick?"

"Yeah. So sick that they gave you the last sacraments." I've been telling her these details several times a day.

"They did? Did they call you kids?"

"Mhmmmm. We were all really scared."

"Was I ranting and raving? Is it time to eat? Are you hungry? What time is it?"

I breathe deeply…I have learned that sometimes it helps to change the subject, but only if I stay right there with something visible or tangible. So I lift a vase of flowers from on top of the dresser and bring it close to her. "Look at your bouquet, Mom. Aren't those yellow daisies from Dick's yard pretty?"

But today's merry-go-round is not about to stop. Sometimes distraction works and sometimes it does not.

"What day is it? Have I been up yet today?"

I can get impatient and irritable listening to the same questions over and over again. The other day, before I could catch myself, I shouted at Mom, which of course did not help the situation. When I answer with an edge, it makes her feel bad, and me too. I ask for the grace of patience at such times, and for the grace of forgiveness—Mom's and my own—when I lose it. Calling on *maitri*…

During conversations like this, I catch a deeper glimpse of what it must be like living inside a mind that is withering away. So many questions swirl around with nowhere to land. Usually, there is no one to answer them, so do they just keep swirling? No wonder Mom is agitated and confused. What a relief it must be to ask the questions aloud and have someone answer.

Only momentary relief, however. For any answers simply bounce off her planet.

Only the questions circle round and around again…

Inside and out…

Answers, Answers

My sister Mary has created a routine that works in a situation like "Questions, Questions," one that helps her remain patient and stay involved. Instead of getting aggravated when Mom is repetitive, Mary tries to see the repeated questions as a challenge to *herself,* to her own creativity. She finds many different ways to answer the same question.

Here's an example:

Mom: "Does your knee hurt?"

Mary: "No, it doesn't."

"You're limping. Does your knee hurt?"

"Oh, not much."

"Does your knee hurt?"

"Only when I move it."

"Does your knee hurt you?"

"I don't know. Maybe I'll get up and see." Mary stands up and walks around the room a bit.

"Does it hurt now?"

"I think I could do a jig." And she does.

I have seen Mary in action on this one, and my sister finds it amazingly effective in keeping her from becoming impatient or frustrated. Rather, smiling and animated, Mary remains genuinely interested in the conversation, and so does Mom—usually. If by chance the jig does not take Mom on a

different track, Mary tries to change the subject—to something concrete—to the TV or a photo album or looking at
something out the window.

Otherwise, Mom's questions can outlast even Mary's en-
durance.

THE SECOND CHALLENGE:
Self-Care and Pacing Myself

*"When we truly care for ourselves, it becomes possible to
care far more profoundly about other people.*

*"The more alert and sensitive we are to our own needs,
the more loving and generous we can be toward others."*
EDA LESHAN

"Someone's Stealing My Stuff"

One morning I call Mom from this summer's home across the
river, and all she will talk about is "Someone's stealing my
stuff! Now my blue robe is gone!"

"I will look for it when I come over this afternoon, Mom," I
promise, being careful not to feed the paranoia. I have my own
suspicions, though. Earlier in the week she had confided, "I'm
going to hide some of my best stuff so it won't be stolen."

Sure enough, this afternoon, after a short search, we find

Mom's favorite robe, hidden—rolled up under the green afghan in the bottom drawer of her dresser. "I didn't put it there!" she swears. "People have been stealing my stuff!"

I do not say much. How sad I am to see Mom, such a loving and trusting woman, becoming suspicious of everyone.

"I'm just a nuisance," she goes on, setting the tone for our hours together.

As we are watching *Wheel of Fortune*, Mom looks over at me, without preface but with great clarity and emphasis, and declares, "Maybe you need a day of your own tomorrow, Rita."

I am stunned. She will not elaborate.

A short time later, her mood turns even more sour. "I just hate this place," she insists, and returns to obsessing about the stealing. She frequently complains of this to me over the phone, and when I visit, she often shoves the hangers together in the closet pointing and complaining, "Look! Nearly everything of mine is gone! They wait 'til I'm out of the room, then someone comes in and steals my stuff! I'm just not going out of this room again!"

"It is true, Mom, your closet is seldom as you leave it." I feel the need to confirm this. Then I add, "Since you don't put your laundry out, the laundry people do have to go through your things to find your dirty clothes." I refrain from finishing the sentence with "…that you hide." Explaining does not help, I know. But I forget and try anyway.

"I just hate this place!" she repeats.

(Breathe, Rita, breathe.)

"It's getting dark, Mom, about time for me to go." I try to distract her, so she will focus on something else. "What about our time together today? Did you enjoy having lunch and watching *Wheel of Fortune*?"

"Well, I just hate this place. I look out the window and all I see is bare air." Then accusingly, "Besides, why do you leave now when this is the hardest part of the night?"

(Whew! Really breathe, Rita, breathe.)

I bite my tongue to keep from saying, *After spending six and a half hours together today, that is all you have to say when I leave?*

My attitude is showing. I do not like it, but there it is. It is time to call on *maitri*, once again. To be gentle to myself.

And to acknowledge my feelings. How helpless I feel tonight, how frustrated. Sometimes it seems like nothing I do or say makes a difference. It is days like these that I do question whether my being back here in the Midwest for the summer is a comfort to Mom. Often I do not even know that. And yet, after a good night's sleep, I realize that I am bound to feel this way at times. Isn't that an integral part of pilgrimage, walking together no matter what? I do not have to change Mom or anybody else. Just myself.

So what can I do to change myself? More than anything, I need to accept Mom where she is—and accept my own limitations as well. I once heard another caregiver explain to a fellow elevator-rider, "There is nothing I can do for him, and I am doing it."

I take comfort in those words.

⸂⸂⸉

"Maybe You Need a Day All Your Own"

Driving home last night in a rather sour frame of mind my-self, I was pondering Mom's curious words earlier that after-noon: "Maybe you need a day of your own tomorrow."

Where did that thought, that declaration, come from? I won-der. Could it be that *Mom* needs a break from *me*, and that is her way of saying it? It never occurred to me that she might need a break as much as I. Maybe she wants to take a nap, not "do" so much, not be "on" so much—although I don't think she feels she has to be "on" with me. Whatever it is, the com-ment surprises me.

It occurs to me that I really do want Mom to appreciate my efforts. But, realistically, can she? Much of her memory is gone, and much of what I know as my mother has disappeared. My expectations of her—and of myself—are often too high. I am not perfect. I do get angry. I do lose my patience. I've had to use *maitri* a lot lately.

I need to forgive myself, and forgive Mom as well. I need to acknowledge what I do that is helpful, rather than harp on the ways I fail to meet my high expectations. I guess that is one way of taking care of myself. Every pilgrim needs to do that in order to keep going on the journey.

Well, although I am here for the summer, to spend as much time as possible with Mom, perhaps I do need a break. I have not missed a day since I arrived. Hmmmmm, that's seven weeks. I do need to take care of myself, to pace myself a bit more. Now that I think of it, a timeout would be refreshing.

Maybe Mom is right. Maybe I do need a day all my own...

I take it.

THE THIRD CHALLENGE:
Being Flexible and Letting Go

The art of being wise is the art of knowing what to overlook.
WILLIAM JAMES

Knowing What Matters

"Tonight is the barbershop quartet, Mom. Dick and I will be over after supper to pick you up!"

"Oh, I love barbershop quartets!"

We know that. That's why Dick and I have been planning this event for several days. Dick has the folding chairs and the cushions in the car—we have packed all the necessities. I've made certain Mom has a sweater, and a thin head scarf, and anything else she might need. I have checked it all out and gotten an okay from Kahl Home.

As we pick Mom up, the Home's monthly "Cocktail Party" is about to begin. "Gee, there's free booze," Mom laughs, mockingly regretful, as we walk out the door. There is that familiar sense of humor coming through, a spark from better days. I treasure those rare moments when it creeps back.

Dick drives to Lincoln Park, a forested hilly area of the city. Hundreds of people have come out for the occasion, and we have to park at quite a distance. Dick and I hang chairs over one arm, leaving the other free for Mom to hold on to. I load up my backpack as well, and the three of us slowly negotiate the steep flights of stairs, one at a time, up to the concert area.

Whew! Stopping to catch our breath at the top of the steps, we look around for just the right spot, especially one where Mom will have a clear view of the stage. We choose a grassy place under an enormous oak tree, and settle ourselves comfortably, ready to be entertained.

Mom is seldom outside at night anymore, and she is in awe. She keeps gazing all around, marveling, "Look at these trees. Aren't they beautiful? And the branches hang out so far. Down so low..."

At last the concert begins. The first quartet performs two numbers. We in the audience can see their mouths moving, but we cannot hear a thing. Technicians come up to the stage and tinker with the equipment, but to no avail. Five more quartets cycle through the program, which, for us, has become mostly lip synch with scarcely a sound—except for the system's periodic screeches and crackles. Nevertheless, Mom is tapping her foot and swaying to the music each time she hears even snatches.

Dick and I, on the other hand, tap only one foot—to a different beat, impatient and irritated. For us, the erratic, crackly static ruins the entire event. We stay perhaps an hour, then leave in frustration, inching our way in the dark, through the thinning crowd and across the grass. Back down the stairs we trudge, where Mom and I wait, tending all our paraphernalia until Dick comes with the car.

As consolation, Dick drives us on a tour of the city lights. Mom is enchanted. "Oh, that's such a pretty building at night!"

"Oooo, what are all those lights?"

"That's the baseball diamond, Mom," Dick explains.

We pass tall majestic homes and tiny hovels. Mom admires all the street lights that are "so pretty." Even the colors of the traffic lights draw her attention, although she does not recognize them as such. "Isn't that a pretty green!" she says.

"It is!" I am almost shocked. I had never noticed the vibrancy of that traffic-light green before tonight.

We pull into the Kahl Home driveway around 9:30 P.M. or so, and Dick and I are yawning and fading fast. As we approach her room, I ask, "Are you tired, Mom?"

"Not at all!" she replies—and it's true. There is still a jaunt to her step. Being out in nature always revitalizes Mom, especially with the bonus of being with her kids. And, dare I say, I suspect what energized her most tonight was just "going with the flow."

It didn't matter much to Mom that she could not hear the singing of the barbershop quartets. Dick and I, on the other hand, became restless early on in the concert, frustrated by the faulty sound system. It had to be a certain way for us. We had to get what we expected. I think that is partly what drained our energy and made us so tired.

But Mom had been utterly content. Outside, in the cool summer night air, under huge gorgeous trees. Just sitting between her two eldest—at times leaning over and whispering in our ears or reaching out to touch our hands, drinking in the love.

Nothing else mattered.

Donuts

"Of course I go down to coffee on Saturdays," Mom tells me.

I take her at her word, saying, "Let's go!"

She looks at me blankly. "Go where?"

"Down for coffee and donuts. It's Saturday morning."

"Oh, I've never gone down for coffee and donuts on Saturday morning."

"Well, shall we go down and see what it's like?"

We do. I totally ignore the issue of whether she has done this before, because it doesn't matter. "Facts" for Mom seem to change from one minute to the next, and I have to be flexible if I am to relate gently to Mom. What can I do to keep from contradicting Mom? From arguing about what the "facts" are in any given situation? In the past, I've not been proud of myself in this arena. It is not easy to bite my tongue when all I want to do is "set matters straight."

The first thing I must remember to do in a "Donuts" situation is STOP. Just STOP—and catch my breath. Yes, stop. Breathe. Let my imagination go to work, walk in Mom's shoes for a moment. Try to figure out what might be worrying her, given the current scenario.

For instance, in this "Donuts" situation, I imagine that something like this might be going on in Mom's mind: *I'm scared of going down there. Will I remember what to do? Am I supposed to bring donut money? Where is my purse? Where is my money? I don't have any money. What time does it start? Will I know anybody there? What if I spill the coffee? What if I have to go to the bathroom? How close is it?* Anxiety is written all over her face.

There is no way to know if Mom actually asks herself any of these questions, but ruminating along these lines helps *me*. It slows me down—and can bring me to a compassionate place if I let it. Then I can ask myself, *How can I help Mom save face and feel good about herself?* Surprisingly, it takes only a few seconds to figure this out.

I must keep reminding myself: it's our relationship that counts. Not the facts. The caring.

As I think about it, I realize there are countless occasions that call for the "Donuts" strategy. For instance, some of my most uncomfortable moments with Mom have been when she says to me, "I'm going home next week." This is real. She believes it with all her heart.

If I were to respond to her words with "facts" from my point of view, I would say something like, "Now Mom, you know you can't go back home. You know the house is sold."

What a foul mood words like these can bring on! Mom becomes depressed, agitated, angry, and all it does is stir up argument and resentment between us. Neither one of us feels good.

So when Mom tells me, "I'm going home next week," I have tried various responses: I've said,

"Oh, I bet you would love to go home, Mom," or

"Wouldn't that be wonderful!" or

"That is such a sweet little house, isn't it," or

"There was always lots of love in our house, lots of laughing."

Such responses are honest, and open another kind of door, one that can engage Mom in talking about the house, about memories, rather than obsessing about going home. And we are both the happier for it. I simply must respond to Mom's feelings around the subject, and try to dodge any arguing about who is right. I avoid any contradicting, while remaining truthful.

Of course, I do not manage to respond from this place 100 percent of the time. (Remember *maitri* at those times.) However, when I am fortunate enough to be graced with "Donuts" awareness, I have been guided and coached by Naomi

Feil's book *The Validation Breakthrough*—a helpful resource for this kind of validating process. She suggests some key questions to ask, such as

— What is going on inside Mom?
— What is true for her?
— What response will help Mom feel good about herself?
— What response nurtures the relationship between the two of us at this moment?

I have come to the conclusion that it is disrespectful, condescending, and even arrogant to try convincing Mom (or anyone else for that matter) that her reality is "off." As if mine were the only true one. There are so many ways to be right, so many ways to be wrong—and on so many levels.

Is it possible that two seemingly contradictory realities can dance together rather than butt heads? Yes, I think so. It's a matter of respect. Letting go. Being flexible. Not having to be right—all vital companions in walking one another home.

The Hardest Time of the Night

It is after ten o'clock when Mom and I return from the Celebrant Singers concert. In all the nearby rooms, the lights are out. We inch our way down the long hall, past darkened rooms. Snores and groans punctuate the heavey silence. After we hug in her doorway with the familiar, "'Nite, 'nite. Don't let the bed bugs bite," I take a few steps toward the elevator. As I turn to wave, Mom and I begin blowing silly, loud kisses, complete with smacking sounds, back and forth to each other down the hallway, followed by a loudly whispered, "I love you."

It seems I say good-bye to my mother in bits and pieces. How I long for such a simple pleasure: to go about getting ready for bed and turning in like we used to all those years when I visited her at home, calling back and forth to each other until we fell asleep. Under the same roof, we would wake up to morning coffee and the start of another day. I never realized how sweet it was—sharing common everyday activities—until such sharing was no longer possible.

How it tugs at my heart every time I leave Mom behind in this place called "The Home." I always look back to see her slight, lone figure hunched at the end of a long hallway. Just down the hall. But on the other side of a great abyss. The Alzheimer abyss.

Sometimes we can reach across the chasm, and sometimes we cannot.

A few evenings ago, Mom complained, "You always leave me at the hardest time of the night." It might be 6 P.M. or 8 P.M. or 10 P.M. At whatever time we part—that automatically becomes "the hardest time of the night." It is when we have had our together time, and now we must go our separate ways, each keenly aware of how alone she is, how confused, and how utterly lost.

Nevertheless, I must leave. And I do. It is not guilt I feel anymore when we part. It's more a deep sadness, a resigned helplessness.

Yes, there she is, smiling as I leave. Being playful, while her heart is sinking. (Mine too.) Being brave—and scared—all in one. (Me too.) And trusting—that's a tough one for me here: entrusting her care to someone else.

I want to run back and hug her again. Hold her tightly. Remind her how much I love her. Tell her that everything's going to be all right in the midnight darkness descending all around her.

But is it? I cannot promise that to her—or to myself. So I resist.

(Breathe, Rita, breathe.)

With one final wave, I disappear around the corner.

How long, I wonder, does she linger at her doorway, peering around it, after I have gone?

Ninety-Second Birthday

We (Mom's five "kids") have gathered together from the four corners of the country for a family reunion celebrating Mom's ninety-second birthday.

"When is my birthday?" she asks.

"It's September 28th! We are all here to celebrate!"

"How old am I now?"

"You're ninety-two, Mom!"

"Ninety-two?" she marvels, and counters with, "Why, no one should be let loose at that age." Mom's sense of humor flashes most unexpectedly these days. It is amazing how she can still rise to the occasion.

Looking at my brother Jerry, she asks, "Who's that guy?"

"I'm Jerry," he explains, "in from California."

"Oh," she pretends. "I knew that. I was just kidding."

She goes on to ask him, "So did you invite Dad to this birthday party?"

We all think she means *our* dad, her Farley. Before Jerry can respond, though, Mom adds, "Did you invite my mom and dad?"

Jerry, without skipping a beat, responds, "Well, I didn't know you wanted them to come."

"Well sure, they always come to our celebrations."

An art we Bresnahans fine-tuned when we were growing up is how to celebrate, how to throw a party. The five of us go shopping together at the nearby mall. We find a perfect bouquet of flowers, with tiny pink roses and baby breath. We choose cards, silly ones mainly, and one "mushy" one, and we buy a bouquet of multi-colored helium balloons. One shouts "Happy Birthday," one simply says "Mom," and a heart-shaped one whispers "I Love You."

On the Big Day, Mom dresses up in the soft tan sweatshirt Patti had custom-made for the previous Mother's Day. The word "Mom" is scripted in large maroon letters across the front of the sweatshirt, and stitched underneath the word "Mom" are three blue and three maroon hearts, each bearing the name of one of her "kids." Mom sports a red top hat with "Happy Birthday" printed on the brim, and on cue, she tips her hat with gusto.

During the noon birthday feast of roast beef—Mom's favorite—I conduct a mock interview, inquiring, "How did you get to be ninety-two, Madam?"

"Well," she says, "the calendar didn't break down."

Several times, I remind Mom who each of us is, by name, referring to each as one of her "wonnnnnderful children."

"Is that a joke?" she asks. Which makes us all laugh.

When it's time for the family birthday party, the five of us, along with Mom, form a "birthday parade." We fasten a couple of birthday balloons to the back of the wheelchair. Mom's youngest daughter, Patti, like a drum majorette, leads us all, holding high the special chocolate cake with roses, with Mom's picture lasered into the icing. Out from Mom's room, we parade down the hall, into the elevator, then out onto the patio, where we have set up the celebration. The afternoon sky is a bit overcast, and a slight breeze periodically whips corners of the tablecloths up and over the table edges.

Patti sets the cake in the center of the table and puts candles on it. We have brought party cups with the name "Miriam" on them. Birthday napkins and plates matching the tablecloths complete the festive setting. With Mom directing, we sing "Happy Birthday," and all help blow out the candles. We sing other songs as well, old favorites like "Roll Out the Barrel," "Harvest Moon," and "When Irish Eyes Are Smiling." Usually we can count on singing to engage Mom, but today she chimes in with only a word here and there, in stark contrast to former days when she would bellow out every word of the lyrics in her wonderfully strong alto voice.

When we finish cleaning up after the party, we push Mom's wheelchair out onto the grass at the top of the knoll overlooking the Mississippi River. As the five of us cluster around her, there is an air of awe, of specialness, of needing to savor each moment. Mom comes amazingly alive. "It's always so still," she whispers, looking quietly up into her beloved trees.

When it begins to get chilly, the five of us stroll with Mom all around Kahl Home grounds, taking turns pushing the wheelchair. "The pusher" often is lightly touching or massaging Mom's shoulders when we are at a standstill. She loves this touch. "Mmmmm," she murmurs, "that feels good!" With birthday balloons billowing in the late afternoon breeze, we stop by all Mom's favorite haunts. First the grotto, where each of us takes a turn sitting in front of the Blessed Virgin statue with her. After stopping to say hello to the marigolds and petunias along the driveway, we move on to the chapel. Our pilgrimage has an eerie feel to it, almost like a farewell parade as well as a birthday stroll.

As we stop by the front desk on the way back into the home, Mom tips her birthday hat to Evie, the receptionist, whose face lights up. "Miriam, your smile always makes my day!" Evie declares–and she means it. That is how a lot of people respond to Mom.

After we wheel back up to Mom's room and the others take off to pick up supper somewhere, I spend a half hour alone with Mom so she can rest. Suddenly, she points to her TV and asks, "Is that empty?" Looking around at the walls, she adds, "And they changed all the pictures in this room on me!"

What does she see? I wonder. The photographs are in their usual places, as far as I can tell. There is Dad's picture on the wall, Dick's photos from Israel, and all of our graduation pictures in their tiny gold frames sit on her dresser. So what does she see? It strikes me that all of her inner pictures must be shifting, changing. Rapidly, moment by moment.

I decide to push Mom in her wheelchair to the lounge so we can sit at our favorite windows and look out toward the Mississippi. Or what is usually our favorite spot. Today she scarcely notices. Perhaps she is overtired. It has been a long day.

Gazing out the window, Mom initiates "conversation" in a flat, disembodied voice that I have not heard before: "I saw a woman really fighting to get out of here. She's scared. She says things and they don't make any sense. Right afterwards they took her away, and nobody knows where they took her. A lot of people just go crazy here, and you don't know what to do. You don't know how much they're going to take. They either lock you in or tie you up. I came near leaving. They're prepared better than I realized....Sure. Sure. There, there. Now don't get too scared. Don't run away. Stay here…There's no place to go….Sure. Sure. That's all right…. Poor people. They look so scared."

I am stunned. Mom utters all this without a pause, as if no one else is there, saying aloud what must incessantly be whirring around in her mind.

(*Breathe, Rita, breathe.*)

In an attempt to connect with her somewhere, I pick up on her last words, "Are *you* scared, Mom?"

She only continues the monologue, compulsively rubbing her fingers up and down along the folds in the drapes. "She was asking me what's the matter with this? And I said the hallway was loose… So I found it for her and gave it to her. That's all we've had since then…. The only thing they tell me is doing something. So she writes when she goes away. I try to keep track of it, but it's wasted on me."

I do not know what to say. I'm having trouble breathing. I attempt to draw Mom back, using her own famous lines: "Aren't the trees beautiful?" Almost as a courtesy, she glances out the window toward the Mississippi. "That's pretty. Everything is so big." Then her mood shifts visibly. Her eyes strain to see across the rooftops out to the river. "There's all that gas out there. It's so sharp and dangerous. The war's starting all over. The war. See the guns! And the poor little kids…." Long pause. "The trees are really mad today. The wind is blowing all those boxes. Blowing. Blowing red. They're wet, but they let out red, and red blows all over."

Red sweeps into the room and knocks all the wind out of me. It fills my nostrils and makes my eyes burn. All my resolve to stay in the present, to look with fresh eyes...swept away with *red* blowing, blowing. I too feel lost, whirring. Caught up in *red*. *Red* is everywhere, so thick I cannot breathe.

Where are Patti and Mary and Dick and Jerry? Where are they? Why don't they come back? What is taking them so long? For one of the first times ever I find myself fidgeting, teary, anxious to have the company of others here, instead of relishing being alone with Mom.

My heart is heavy. All day I have been able to hold the heaviness at bay, but now it weighs on me, confronting me with its undeniable presence. Might this be Mom's last birthday? We kids had whispered the possibility to one another over the phone. Seeing her now, I am convinced. I am appalled, heartsick at the deterioration in Mom's condition just since Mother's Day. That is only four months.

Especially alarming is that Mom has forgotten how to eat. She stops mid-bite, uncertain whether her fork should go up or down. Or she takes a bite of food and does not like the texture or the flavor (is there any?) or does not recognize what she's eating. "What is that?" she asks, removing a mushroom from her mouth. Today she just dabbed at her birthday feast, swallowing perhaps three tiny bites of roast beef and a pinch of mashed potatoes. And each of those only after great coaxing and some assistance from one of us.

Mom seems not to enjoy food anymore—not even her

perennial favorite, butter-pecan ice cream, that we had had with her birthday cake. She simply did not know what to do with ice cream on a spoon.

"Put it into your mouth, Mom," Patti had coached. But Mom did not know what direction that meant. "Into your mouth!" She swirled the spoon a bit and smiled. The spoon hung in midair, ice cream melting, splattering onto the maroon "Mom" of her sweatshirt.

Mom cannot live long without eating, this I know. She is wasting away, and I am desperate to persuade her to eat. At noon I had tried several ruses to encourage her to sip her Ensure, the nutritional supplement served with each meal.

"Raise your glasses everybody! Let's toast Mom's birthday!" (Clink! Sip!)

"Let's toast each one of your kids, Mom!" (Clink, sip! Clink, sip...)

"To this sunny day!" (Clink! sip!)

We remember old favorite recipes that Mom used to make, and we "clink, sip" after each delicious one. "Take a sip now, Mom."

We toast anything we can think of, creating excuses to raise our glasses and have Mom follow suit, sipping her elixir. She makes a valiant effort, but little nourishment goes down.

Yes, I am desperate to get Mom to eat. Desperate.

A chill suddenly comes over me, a chill bearing this indisputable message: *Her body is shutting down.*

Oh no!

Oh yes. This is her rhythm. Honor her rhythm. Do not push.
You're pushing too hard.

But she is my mother!

You've got to let go.

But she's my mother!

Let go. There's nothing you can do.

But she's...

Let go.

(Breathe, Rita, breathe.)

Happy Birthday, Mom.

Let go.

Happy Birthday, Mom...

Happy Birthday.

Chapter Six

KINDLY LIGHT

"Lead, Kindly Light—
amid th'encircling gloom, lead Thou me on.
The night is dark and I am far from home...."
CARDINAL JOHN HENRY NEWMAN

Lead, Kindly Light

The time has come for me to leave. Tomorrow, with great reluctance, I return to Seattle. This last night, Mom and I are moving slowly along the Alzheimer's floor toward the elevator, holding hands the way we often do. Slightly behind me as we round the curve at the nurses' station, Mom whispers, "Lead, kindly light." I turn back toward her, straining to hear what she has said. Her eyes flash a remarkable light from some deep ancient Miriam place. She just dances our hands forward, repeating "Lead, kindly light."

We both stop in our tracks and simply stand for an eternal moment gazing at each other, cradled in a meeting place beyond words, speaking volumes. We squeeze each other's hand, keenly aware of our profound relationship—far beyond mother-daughter blood ties.

Not only do we know with a certainty that we are bathed in Kindly Light, we each lead at different times. I, usually through physical space now; Mom, at other times. Each honoring and trusting the other's lead, each letting ourselves be seen, and seeing each other as we have seldom before allowed.

"Lead, Kindly Light." From which file in Mom's great but swiftly dwindling storehouse of memory did she excavate those words? Although they are vaguely familiar to me, I have never heard Mom speak them. I begin wondering, *Is that the title of a hymn, a poem—or what?* I must find out.

When I get back to Seattle, I call the local library and ask for help. "We'll have the piece found for you by the time you get here," I am assured.

Sure enough, when I arrive, the librarian holds open a book of sacred music. "Here it is!" she beams. "It's a poem by Cardinal John Henry Newman, set to music and sung on special religious occasions."

I sit down at a nearby table and read the full text, marveling, feeling goose bumps as I reflect on the poem's rich symbolism. If "Kindly Light" here means "God" in Mom's theology, then this hymn paints the story of Mom's faithfulness to her God as she walked the peaks and the valleys of her life.

> *"Lead, Kindly Light—*
> *amid th'encircling gloom, lead Thou me on.*
> *The night is dark..."*

These days, Mom is indeed encircled by gloom, by the Alzheimer fog closing in around her, besieging her. She lives in many darknesses—of her ruthless fears, of her confusion, of her paranoia, of her memory loss. Twilight hours seem the most wrenching, as she becomes acutely aware that she is disappearing into the shadows.

> *"Lead, Kindly Light—*
> *...the night is dark, and I am far from home...."*

Mom *is* far far from home. From her sweet home of sixty years, her home overlooking the lake she loved so dearly and walked so joyfully. From the heart-home she shared with Dad for twenty-eight years. From her inside-Miriam home of over ninety years.

> *"Lead, Kindly Light—*
> *...I loved to choose and see my path..."*

For most of her life, Mom has been able both to see and choose the path ahead. As a young woman, she chose to marry Farley, to have a large family, to live the Catholic faith. She chose to learn to drive. She made such seemingly simple daily choices that we all take for granted: what clothes to wear, what to cook for supper, what to watch on TV, whom to call on the telephone, when to go to the bathroom.

Gradually Mom's choices have dwindled. She never dreamed that she would have to leave her Pekin home. Never could she have imagined herself in a nursing home. How fiercely she fought these major decisions that she did not make but rather *were made for* her.

And now even the smallest everyday choices are outside of her control.

"Lead, Kindly Light...I was not always thus,
    nor prayed that Thou shouldst lead me on..."

Even in the years before Alzheimer's struck, Mom had not always been in a peaceful, trusting place. Not always did she pray for her Kindly Light to lead her on. In fact, years were when she ranted and raved at God, feeling betrayed by Farley's early death, prematurely making her a widow. Raising two tender young girls by herself, while weighed down by deep mourning seemed unbearable.

Amazingly, Mom made it through this tough passage, somehow gathering strength through it all. I can still see her jaw set, her teeth clenched in stubborn resolve, determined to rule her own life. After fighting so hard to establish her independence, should it be surprising now that she lashes out in anger when it seems taken away at every turn?

"Lead, Kindly Light—
...So long Thy pow'r hath blest me,
Sure it will lead me on..."

Mom's faith did return. Even in the midst of darkness, she continues to stand in God's Light, in the strength of that fervent and solid faith. In earlier years, Mom would passionately sing the words of her favorite hymn: "...I will raise you up on eagle's wings...and hold you in the palm of my hand." Even now, although the words are gone, they continue to express her surrender to God's lead.

At some level, Mom must know how blest she is: with her kids' love, with the grace of attending daily Mass and saying the rosary. Then there's the relief of feeling safe, of not having to worry about meals or a roof leaking or how to get where she needs to go. And how comforting is the consistent, gentle care she receives at Kahl Home.

"Lead, Kindly Light—
...And with the morn those angel faces smile,
which I have loved long since, and lost a while..."

Mom has always been confident that "with the morn"—when her soul is released from this dark night—she will meet her "angel faces" again: her beloved husband, Farley, will be there on the other side to greet her. Her son Bob, too. Her dear parents. All her loved ones who have gone before her.

And she knows she will at last meet her God, her Kindly Light.

> *Face-to-face.*
> *There is no darkness here…*
>
> *Yes… Lead, Kindly Light…*
> *lead Thou her on…*
>
> *and lead Thou me on as well…*

The Ending

Miriam Bresnahan slipped peacefully away
on November 16, 2000,
her priest-son Dick at her bedside.
We buried Mom between her beloved husband, Farley,
and her faithful son Bob,
in St. Joseph's Cemetery, Pekin, Illinois.

PART III

❧

HOME, FROM THE JOURNEY

Miriam Bresnahan leaping for joy on receiving a new car for her eightieth birthday.

Miriam on an excursion to the gambling boat.

Chapter Seven

THE RETURN

Gifts to Me and Gifts to Share

A nd so I return. Grieving months pass...

Then, at some point, I begin pondering one of the questions pilgrims ask when they return home: What gifts do I bring back with me—gifts that deepen my own spiritual life?

At times, I find myself flashing back to the day after Mom's funeral, vividly remembering our bereft family walking sadly, slowly, out of the nursing home, nearly empty-handed. As I looked around marveling that we could carry Mom's meager belongings to the car easily in a single trip, an unsettling thought struck me: *After such a long rich lifetime, this is all there is?*

It is true. Mom had neither expensive belongings nor even a single dollar to bequeath us. Our sole inheritance, her legacy:

a lifetime of teaching us how to walk one another home, with love.

For this gift, I count myself rich beyond measure.

Each of us also possesses a few family mementos. Back in Seattle, I wander through each room of my house, gently touching some of Mom's "treasures" that have become mine over the years. There's a charcoal Scottie dog Mom sketched when she was nineteen. A "Welcome" sign with apple blossoms she hand-crafted. The golden pyx in which she carried communion wafers when she was a eucharistic minister for nursing homes. Tiny teddy bears. Crocheted doilies.

My eyes gaze even more intently on five special keepsakes that symbolize inner gifts I bring back with me: a silver bell with "Niagara Falls" embossed on its handle; a tiny glass bluebird; a wooden olive; a beat-up compass; and an alabaster lamp. Caressing them fondly, I hold each one of these for a moment, reflecting on the healing grace of their messages.

A Silver Bell

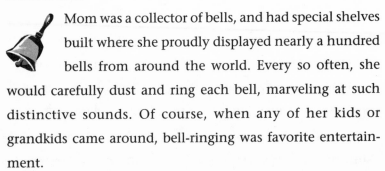Mom was a collector of bells, and had special shelves built where she proudly displayed nearly a hundred bells from around the world. Every so often, she would carefully dust and ring each bell, marveling at such distinctive sounds. Of course, when any of her kids or grandkids came around, bell-ringing was favorite entertainment.

The silver bell that is now mine was Mom's first and dearest, a honeymoon memento. To her this Niagara Falls bell spoke of love, commitment, and faithfulness. For me, it also symbolizes "the ring of mindfulness," a phrase the Buddhist priest Thich Nhat Hanh uses to mean "awaken from forgetfulness." Stay in the present moment.

As I began my pilgrimage, I needed to wake up, for I was losing parts of myself to endless ruminating on the haunting question, "Will Alzheimer's be my fate as well?" This fear permeated my thoughts, disturbed my sleep, even depressed me at times. A friend of mine admitted that it was one of her deepest concerns as well. "How can I prepare?" she asked me. I had no answer for her.

Ultimately, I had to ask myself another question: *Am I undertaking this pilgrimage for my mother's sake—or is it for myself as well?* That answer was clear: I really need to change myself. Handle things differently. Look at things differently. Bring to a halt my growing tendency to withdraw. Somehow transform my downward spiraling thoughts and fears.

For starters, I had to monitor my thoughts, my self-talk, the kind of energies I was projecting—a crucial first step toward waking up, toward preparing for and dealing with this challenge—or any eventuality. That is the ring of mindfulness I most needed. I began to see ways I participated in, and even generated, my own grief. Could I then also generate my own inner peace, and if so, how? That became an integral part of my mission. I realized early on that if I lived my days in fear of the future, I was not fully living. "What if I do get Alzheimer's?" or "What if I take another fall? Then what will happen?"

I could arrive at only one conclusion: To let go of the fear and generate my own peace, I must make a commitment to live each day fully—with as much awareness and love as possible. Not only for the "big stuff," like whether or not I'll get Alzheimer's, but for the small stresses and expectations I put on myself, like wondering *Will I be able to find that house where we are meeting?* or fretting when company's coming: *Is the house clean enough? Will they like what I'm fixing for dinner? What shall I wear?* At times like these, I need to breathe and ask myself, *What really matters here? What really matters?*

If I let Mom's bell remind me to live mindfully each moment, aware of the sacred in my everyday life, then living itself becomes a series of mini-pilgrimages. Each day I set out, as consciously as possible, to visit my own sacred places: my fireplace; my deck; my simple little yard and garden; my car; the office; paths along the water; and wherever I am with loved ones.

And what about the more challenging venues, like the grocery store, the freeway traffic, the laundromat? Aren't these sacred places as well? Yes! And when I forget this truth, I count on Silver Bell to ring out Thich Nhat Hanh's message reminding all pilgrim hearts how to proceed:

"When we hear the Bell of Mindfulness ring,
we stop our thinking,
and we send our hearts along with the sound
　　of the bell.
We breathe in and out three times, saying:
Listen, listen.
This wonderful sound
Brings me back to my true self."
THICH NHAT HANH, *BEING PEACE*, P. 105

A Glass Bluebird

A tiny glass bird, barely thumbnail size, resides on my fireplace mantle. Dubbed by Dad "the bluebird of happiness," it looks like a blob of blue glass with lopsided eyes and gross yellow dots glued on for its beak. If you didn't know it was a bluebird, you would never have guessed it. Growing up, we could usually find that wobbly trinket perched contentedly on the kitchen windowsill. Sometimes she would mysteriously appear in other places.

I remember times when, as a little girl, I would be pouting about something and Dad would call out, "Reet, where's that ole bluebird of happiness?" First I'd peek at the kitchen windowsill, and if she wasn't there, I would flit about the house whispering, "Where *is* that bluebird of happiness? Where *is* that bluebird of happiness?" I would search everywhere. Finally, I'd find it (always confident that I would) on a different windowsill, on the circular bookstand, on one of the steps leading upstairs—at some unexpected but obvious place. I would then hold the treasure high and wave it around shouting, "Daddy, I found the bluebird of happiness!"

In the process, my mood miraculously had lifted.

Did Dad ever dream that sixty years later his daughter would be writing about his little game (or was it a game?)? About the impact it had on her? About how she carries its lessons with her? About how this homely bluebird helps her fly? It is amazing how the tiniest thing a person does can make a huge difference in the life of someone else.

Today Bluebird symbolizes for me a deepened and broadened sense that I am responsible for my own life, my own happiness. As Bluebird teaches me, I hold that key to my own life in my own hands. I return from my pilgrimage with the profound gift of being able to see this connection: *when I remember to be grateful I am joyful*—independent of what is actually happening in my life. And happiness may not be found where I expect it. But it is right in front of me, so easy to find, if I but welcome what is there.

When I am grateful I am joyful. Every day, then, I find my heart filling up and spilling over with gratefulness for the abundance in my life. I take nothing for granted anymore. Nothing. My health, my memory, my eyesight, my family, my friends. The work I am able to do. Each is so precious.

I begin each day simply, gently, as if opening the door to a sacred space. Even on those days I wake up feeling frightened or alone or empty, I still declare my gratefulness for the light of another morning. No matter what my mood, I raise my arms above my head whispering—or sometimes shouting—"Thank you for my life. Thank you for this day." The same simple prayer ends my day as I speak aloud its many blessings.

> *"If the only prayer we ever say is thank you,*
> *that is enough."*
> MEISTER ECKHART

A Wooden Olive

A wooden olive may seem a strange relic to bring back with me, but it holds a special significance.

Our family was poor when I was growing up, right after the Depression years. I know this only retrospectively, for as a young girl I didn't realize it.

During one of our visits twenty years ago or so, Mom asked me out of the blue, "Rita, do you feel like you had a deprived childhood?"

I was shocked. "That is the last word I would use to describe those years, Mom!"

But I was curious. "What makes you ask me that question?"

She could hardly get the words out. "Well, you, you... we never had... olives..."

I had to repress a laugh, for Mom was so serious. She reminded me that Minnie and Joe, our next-door neighbors, always had olives—especially for their martinis—but no jar of olives ever reached our family's table. With so many kids, the Bresnahans barely had enough money for the basics. So our olive supply line was next-door.

Beginning with that conversation, "The Olive" became a special family mascot. We would send cards or mugs or magnets to Mom, and to one another, with olive caricatures wildly waving "Olive ya." For me, an "olive practice" began to grow out of these exchanges: "Remember to shine the spotlight on what you do have rather than on what you do not." I watched Mom and Dad live that practice fully.

How does that practice translate into my life today? In recent years, there have been times when I've resisted focusing on what I do have. Rather, I find myself demanding back what I *used* to have, *used* to be able to do, especially physically. Holding on stubbornly in this way, refusing to move ahead, not acknowledging the way things are, does not work well for me.

As an active, athletic woman, my social life used to revolve primarily around strenuous outdoor activities like mountain climbing, hiking and backpacking, skiing, and biking—until my late fifties. Then, one by one, these precious sources of great joy, exhilaration, and camaraderie came to a screeching halt. In recent years, I have struggled with arthritis, especially in my knees and hands. Five surgeries so far—and a fractured ankle.

The shrinking of my active lifestyle has been hard to take. At times, I've been angry about these losses, even depressed and withdrawn, especially as I watch my friends continue to take off on their adventures and I'm forced to become more sedentary. I've tried to let go emotionally—but how I yearn to climb mountains again. Each winter I long to cross-country ski and glide along sparkling fresh snow with my buddies.

I catch myself fantasizing…I am back on the trails with them—drinking in the sunshine and the beauty all around, laughing and telling stories… Then suddenly—I'm jolted back to earth, back to the reality of a more couch-potato existence. My mood plummets…

It takes some time to move from that dark place around my physical limitations—especially following each surgery. But it's all part of grieving, I've discovered: I must acknowledge and talk about those yearnings, those angry and depressed feelings too. And yes, I must accept where I am—inside and out. Only at that point might I remember there's an olive practice I can call on to get me back on track.

I wish I could always dwell in a peaceful "olive" place. But my life is not like that. Something can pull me off center in a flash; there are so many triggers. Rigid expectations about the way something is *supposed* to be inevitably trip me up. Assumptions get in my way. Computer snafus drive me wild. Physical challenges too: my hands always have to wrestle with opening a jar. I'm so clumsy—I spill stuff all the time, and I trip over nothing. I can't read words right in front of me, and my glasses are nowhere to be found. I cannot finish a walk I've begun with friends because my knees are hurting so. And at times, I must admit, I still worry about Alzheimer's. I forget how to get somewhere I've been dozens of times before. Often I can't remember a word that's just on the tip of my tongue. I have an increasingly shorter fuse when someone does not understand what I'm trying to say.

Any one of these almost daily challenges frustrates me, makes me anxious or impatient. I fall apart, foolishly trying to control that which cannot be controlled. I fly off the handle—losing my patience at the tiniest stumbling block—and start behaving in ways quite contrary to how I want to live my life. I become defensive. I hurt the feelings of people I care about, and of people I don't even know. Not at home in my spirit, I begin wondering who I am. I become totally disoriented with the discrepancy between how I am behaving and how I want to live. *Maitri* is nowhere to be found.

Then, if I'm lucky, Olive reminds me: "Look, Rita. You can still do so much. You can do your own grocery shopping—you can even walk to the store. You can do the chores you need to do. You can drive. You can work in your garden. You can still walk along the waterfront at sunset. You can do so many things that bring you joy…You can…You can…"

"Yes, but…"

That olive is insistent: "Be grateful for what you *can* do, Rita, for what is still possible, rather than moaning about what you cannot do."

When I remember to breathe and open to a deeper appreciation of what I have now, an abiding gratefulness moves back into this pilgrim heart. "Okay. It's true. How blest I am. How truly blest I am."

Dwell in possibility.
EMILY DICKINSON

A Beat-Up Compass

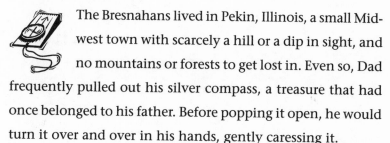 The Bresnahans lived in Pekin, Illinois, a small Midwest town with scarcely a hill or a dip in sight, and no mountains or forests to get lost in. Even so, Dad frequently pulled out his silver compass, a treasure that had once belonged to his father. Before popping it open, he would turn it over and over in his hands, gently caressing it.

Dad often gave us kids compass lessons on how to orient ourselves. Ever so slowly, he would take a step or two around our living room, three or four of us tailing his every move. "See how the arrow quivers and moves when we do...see how it points out each direction...." He especially liked showing us "True North."

I was intrigued by this mysterious gadget. I, too, loved holding it, caressing it. I still do.

So now, when I'm off course, not feeling at home in my spirit, or starting to behave in ways quite contrary to how I want to live, oftentimes a wondrous grace catches me, stops me in my tracks, calls me to attention. It's like Dad's compass reading True North saying, "Rita, stop! That is not who you are, who you want to be. That is not the direction you want to go." And if I but listen to this prompting of the Spirit, I am usually able to stop the negative momentum building up. I can relax, I can pray, I can remind myself of all I've learned on the pilgrimage. And I can shift—shift my behavior, my thoughts, my assumptions. Such is the blessing of awareness, the grace of intention. Of making a different choice.

How do I return to True North at times like this? How do I find my bearings? How do I move back into alignment?

I've tried various ways, depending on my mood. I breathe, first of all. Breathe. Be still. Offer myself *maitri* if I need to. Laugh at myself if I can. In any case, slow down. I might read. Or journal. Listen to some music, sing and hum along. Sit by the water or out in nature somewhere. Or go have some fun. At times I have to do something physical—like go for a walk—either by myself or with someone who really listens, who brings out the best in me. Or I might reach out to someone who's also hurting, and the two of us walk one another home.

And, of course, I call to mind the words of one of the wisest men I've ever known:

> *You can find your way anywhere*
> *if you know where True North is.*
> FARLEY BRESNAHAN

An Alabaster Lamp

Two rose-colored alabaster lamps stood proudly on either side of Mom's vanity dresser, treasures Mom and Dad hand-carried on the train back from their honeymoon. About ten inches tall, each has graceful flourishes and flowers etched on all six sides, and a blossoming tulip provides the handle for their removable lids. All the days of my growing up, their rosy love-light softly illuminated my parents' bedroom every evening.

I fell heir to one of these precious lamps, which today graces the oak shelf at my bedside. Now its rosy hues illuminate my own bedroom each evening. After a long day, I gently turn its switch and settle into the night, murmuring my litany of "thank yous."

Hours later, there it is again, welcoming me as I squint into the morning—my eyes scarcely open. Its presence, its gentle luminescence, its benediction comfort me more than I can say.

This lamp bespeaks the true spiritual nature of pilgrimage, and its message needs little embellishment. From this lamp glows the walking-one-another-home light—the remarkable light we human beings share as we walk with one another. Mom-and-Dad light. Bresnahan light. Love-light. *Namaste* light. *Maitri* light.

And, of course, from this alabaster lamp radiates Amazing Light, ever faithfully abiding behind eyes dulled by Alzheimer's, and in every other place where the light only appears to have gone out. Amazing Light, whose brightness can penetrate even such a darkness, drawing up deep from Mom's soul a fervent but long-forgotten prayer:

"Lead, Kindly Light."

Profound gratitude wells up for these unspeakable gifts that enrich my own spirit, my own life. I am blessed. I am changed. A silver bell, a tiny glass bluebird, a wooden olive, a beat-up compass, and an alabaster lamp. Threads weaving themselves through my days—threads of mindfulness, gratefulness, choices, being responsible for my own happiness, trusting the process, and the slow, patient work of Spirit. Such simple treasures—relics carried back from a sacred place.

• • • • •

Besides asking, "What gifts do I bring back from my pilgrimage that deepen my own spiritual life?" there is a second question returning pilgrims must address: "What gifts do I bring back to share with others?"

This book, with its stories and its many learnings, is the gift I have to share. Joyfully, I offer this gift, although in the midst of writing it, I frequently found myself caught up in a personal anguish that blocked any creative flow for weeks and months at a time. How deeply I have been changed through this labor of love. Blessed, and humbled, by this seven-year process—a pilgrimage all its own.

I realized early in my journey that in walking together in love and sharing with my mother, or with any other human being, there is a reciprocity that enriches the life of both. *Both.* Early on in the journey, as I would leave Seattle to head to the Midwest, it would be with the single purpose of walking my mother home. But it didn't work that way. Rather, I found that not only was I there for my mother, but my mother helped me—and blessed me—in unexpected and unfathomable ways. For me, this is the true meaning of "walking one another home." There is no separation, no distinction, between who is giving and who is receiving. Between who is walking who home. Mom's prophetic words, "Let's just walk one another home," became a sacred calling. A holy reminder.

These stories reflect how truly we are pilgrims together in a world we often don't understand, pilgrims helping one another make it through the journey and reach home again. *Home.* Where we can be our truest Self, where we feel at peace, "at home," connected to ourselves, to one another, and to the Spirit that holds us all. Where life itself is sacred—and we recognize holy places everywhere.

Many people along this path have asked me a seemingly paradoxical question: How could something so stressful and deeply heart-rending as Alzheimer's possibly be a healing gift? Do you really mean that this experience has been an opportunity for you to deepen parts of yourself?

This book is my unequivocal "YES."

SUGGESTED READINGS

Alzheimer's and Caregiver References

Bell, Sherry M., Ph.D. *Visiting Mom: An Unexpected Gift. A Guide for Visiting Elders With Alzheimer's.* (Sedona, Ariz.: Elder Press, 2000.)

Bell, Virginia. *A Dignified Life: The Best Friends Approach to Alzheimer's Care.* (Health Communications, 2002.)

Castleman, Michael, Dolores Gallagher-Thompson, and Naythons. *There's Still a Person in There: The Complete Guide to Treating and Coping with Alzheimer's.* (New York: Putnam & Sons, 1999.)

Feil, Naomi. *The Validation Breakthrough: Simple Techniques for Communicating with People With "Alzheimer's-type Dementia."* (Baltimore: Health Professions Press, Inc., 1993.)

Hooyman, Nancy and Wendy Lustbader. *Taking Care: Supporting Older People and Their Families.* (New York: Free Press; Collier Macmillan, 1986.)

Jones, Moyra. *Gentlecare: Changing the Experience of Alzheimer's Disease in a Positive Way.* (Point Roberts, Wash.: Hartley & Marks, 1999.)

Keck, David. *Forgetting Whose We Are: Alzheimer's Disease and the Love of God.* (Nashville: Abingdon Press, 1986.)

Lustbader, Wendy. *Counting on Kindness: The Dilemmas of Dependency.* (New York: Free Press, 1991.)

Mace, Nancy. *The 36-Hour Day: A Family Guide to Caring for Persons With Alzheimer Disease, Related Dementing Illnesses, and Memory Loss in Later Life.* (Baltimore: Johns Hopkins University Press, 1999.)

Mathiasen, Patrick, M.D. *An Ocean of Time. Alzheimer's: Tales of Hope and Forgetting,* (New York: Simon & Schuster (Scribner), 1997.)

McLeod, Beth Witrogen. *Caregiving: The Spiritual Journey of Love, Loss, and Renewal.* (New York: John Wiley & Sons, 1999.)

Morris, Virginia. *How to Care for Aging Parents: A Complete Guide.* (New York: Workman Publishing, 1994.)

Murphey, Cecil B. *My Parents, My Children: Spiritual Help for Caregivers.* (Louisville, Ky.: Westminster John Knox Press, 2000.)

Robinson, Anne, Beth Spencer, and Laurie White, et al. *Understanding Difficult Behaviors: Some Practical Suggestions for Coping with Alzheimer's Disease and Related Illnesses.* (Ypsilanti, Mich.: Geriatric Education Center of Michigan, 1999.)

Young, Ellen P. and Peter Rabins. *Between Two Worlds: Special Moments of Alzheimer's and Dementia.* (Amherst, N.Y.: Prometheus Books, 1999.)

Zgola, Jitka M. *Care That Works: A Relationship Approach to Persons with Dementia.* (Baltimore: Johns Hopkins University Press, 1999.)

Prime resource: your local Alzheimer's Association, where gracious staff members greet you, ready to assist you in any way. You can also browse, and borrow books or videos from their up-to-date library. Available for the asking is a Master Book List, divided up into helpful categories: Activities, Caregiver Education & Support, Children and Teenagers, Communication, Design/Environment, Family Life Experiences, Grief & Loss, Spirituality, Multicultural/Ethnic, Persons with Memory Loss, and Public Policy/Advocacy.

Aging and Spirituality Resources

Fischer, Kathleen. *Winter Grace: Spirituality and Aging.* (Nashville: Upper Room Books, 1998.)

Lustbader, Wendy, ed. *What's Worth Knowing?* (New York: Jeremy P. Tarcher/Putnam, 2001.)

Maclay, Elise. *Green Winter: Celebrations of Old Age.* (New York: Reader's Digest Press: distributed by Crowell, 1977.)

Moberg, David, ed. *Aging and Spirituality: Spiritual Dimensions of Aging Theory, Research, Practice and Policy.* (New York: Haworth Pastoral Press, 2001.)

Morrison, Ruth, and Dawn Dridan Radtke. *Aging With Joy.* (Mystic, Connecticut: Twenty-Third Publications, 1989.)

Schacter-Shalomi, Zalman and Ronald S. Miller. *From Age-ing to Sage-ing: A Profound New Vision of Growing Older.* (New York: Warner Books, 1997.)

Snowdon, David. *Aging With Grace: What the Nun Study Teaches Us About Leading Longer, Healthier, and More Meaningful Lives.* (New York: Bantam Books, 2001.)

Thibault, Jane. *A Deepening Love Affair: The Gift of God in Later Years.* (Nashville: Upper Room Books, 1993.)

Tournier, Paul. *Learn to Grow Old.* (Louisville, Ky.: Westminister John Knox, 1991.)

Nouwen, Henri. *Aging: The Fulfillment of Life.* (New York: Doubleday, 1974.)

Spirituality Resources

Arrien, Angeles. *The Four-Fold Way.* (San Francisco: Harper, 1993.)

Artress, Lauren. *Walking a Sacred Path: Rediscovering the Labyrinth As a Spiritual Tool.* (New York: Riverhead Books, 1996.)

Baldwin, Christina. *Calling the Circle: The First and Future Culture.* (New York: Bantam Books, 1998.)

Breathnach, Sarah Ban. *Simple Abundance, A Daybook of Comfort and Joy.* (New York: Warner Books, 1995.)

Chodron, Pema. *When Things Fall Apart: Heart Advice for Difficult Times.* (Boston: Shambhala, 2000.) [I recommend all of her writings.]

Chodron, Pema. *The Places that Scare You: A Guide to Fearlessness in Difficult Times.* (Boston: Shambhala, 2001.)

Cousineau, Phil. *The Art of Pilgrimage: A Seeker's Guide to Making Travel Sacred.* (Berkeley: Conari Press, 2000.)

Hart, Thomas. *Spiritual Quest: A Guide to the Changing Landscape.* (New York/Mahwah N.J.: Paulist Press, 1999.)

Kubler-Ross, Elizabeth, and David Kessler. *Life Lessons.* (New York, Scribner, 2000.)

Levine, Stephen. *A Year to Live: How to Live This Year As If It Were Your Last.* (New York: Bell Tower, 1997.)

Morgan, Richard L. *Remembering Your Story: Creating Your Own Spiritual Autobiography.* (Nashville: Upper Room Books, 2002.)

Muller, Wayne. *How, Then, Shall We Live? Four Simple Questions That Reveal the Beauty and Meaning of Our Lives.* (New York: Bantam Books, 1997.)

Nhat Hahn, Thich. *Being Peace.* (Berkeley: Parallax Press, 1988.)

Salzberg, Sharon. *Lovingkindness: The Revolutionary Art of Happiness.* (Boston: Shambhala, 1997.)

Steindl-Rast, David. *Gratefulness, the Heart of Prayer: An Approach to Life in Fullness.* (New York: Paulist Press, 1990.)

York, Sarah. *Pilgrim Heart: The Inner Journey Home.* (Somerset, N.J.: Jossey-Bass, 2001.)

Other Resources

If you have access to the World Wide Web and would like to stay informed about the latest developments in Alzheimer's research, the largest, most timely, and comprehensive English-language Alzheimer's resource is Alzheimers.com (at *www.alzheimers.com*).

Alzheimer's Association
919 North Michigan Ave., Suite 1000 • Chicago, IL 60611-1676
(800) 272-3900 • *www.alz.org*
    The leading organization in the field. Supports families and caregivers of people with Alzheimer's. Chapters nationwide. To reach a twenty-four-hour hotline for referrals, information, problem solving, and counseling support, call (800) 621-0379.

Alzheimer's Disease Education and Referral Center (ADEAR)
Box 8250 • Silver Spring, MD 20907-8250
(800) 438-4380 • *www.cais.net/adear*
    Sponsored by the National Institute on Aging, ADEAR is a national clearinghouse for information on Alzheimer's. Offers information and publications on diagnosis, treatment, caregiving, long-term care, and research.

American Society on Aging
833 Market St., Suite 511 • San Francisco, CA 94103
(415) 974-9600 • *www.asaging.org*
    A national nonprofit organization whose mission is to promote the dignity and well-being of the elderly. It does not deal directly with Alzheimer's disease, but its conferences and publications relate to caregiving and home care.

Family Caregiver Alliance
425 Bush St., Suite 500 • San Francisco, CA 94108
(415) 434-3388, in CA (800) 445-8106 • *www.caregiver.org*

A national nonprofit organization that helps caregivers dealing with adults suffering from memory loss due to Alzheimer's disease and other dementing conditions. It publishes many helpful resources.

Video Respite • *www.europa.com.*
Developed by researchers at the University of Utah, Video Respite produces calming videos for people with Alzheimer's that give respite time to caregivers. The major strength of these tapes is their cultural specificity that may resonate with certain Alzheimer's sufferers. There are tapes designed for Jews, Christians, African-Americans, Canadians, and Hispanics.

General

Bridges, William. *Transitions: Making Sense of Life's Changes.* (Reading, Mass.: Addison-Wesley, 1980.)

Cameron, Julia. *The Vein of Gold: A Journey to Your Creative Heart.* (New York: G.P. Putnam & Sons, 1996.)

Cameron, Julia. *The Artist's Way: A Spiritual Path to Higher Creativity.* (Los Angeles, Calif.: Jeremy P. Tarcher/Perigee, 1992.)

Cousins, Norman. *Anatomy of an Illness As Perceived by the Patient: Reflections on Healing and Regeneration.* (New York: Norton, 1979.)

Klein, Allen. *The Healing Power of Humor: Techniques for Getting Through Loss, Setbacks...and All That Not-So-Funny Stuff.* (New York: Jeremy P. Tarcher/Putnam, 1989.)

Smollin, Ann Bryan. *Tickle Your Soul: live well, love much, laugh often.* (Notre Dame, Ind.: Sorin Books, 1999.)

Periodicals

Generations: Vincennes, Indiana. *www.vinu.edu/generations/magazine.htm.*

Journal of Alzheimer's Disease. Cleveland, Ohio: Institute of Pathology, Case Western Reserve University. *www.j-alz.com.* For inquiries, contact *information@j-alz.com.*

"*Aging and the Human Spirit.*" Galveston, Tex.: A Newsletter, University of Texas Medical Branch, *www.utmb.edu/agingspirit/Newsletter.htm.*

"*The Way Through.*" Hiles, Marv and Nancy, ed. Healdsburg Calif.: Iona Center.